THE
GOD
YOU
CAN
KNOW

THE GOD YOU CAN KNOW

DAN DeHAAN

Foreword by
J. I. Packer

MOODY PUBLISHERS
CHICAGO

*To the apostle Paul, whose single life has encouraged me to
dig deeply into the things of God—and to know Him well.*

© 1982 by
THE MOODY BIBLE INSTITUTE
OF CHICAGO

All Scripture quotations, except those noted otherwise, are from the *New American
Standard Bible*®, © Copyright The Lockman Foundation 1960, 1962, 1963,
1968, 1971, 1972, 1973, 1975, 1977. Used by permission.

Scripture quotations marked KJV are taken from the King James Version.

This book is designed for personal study and enjoyment, but is also well-suited
for use in Bible study groups.

Library of Congress Cataloging-in-Publication Data

DeHaan, Dan.
    The God you can know / Dan DeHaan
        p. cm.
    Originally published: © 1982
    ISBN-10: 0-8024-3007-4
    ISBN-13: 978-0-8024-3007-6
    1. God. I. Title.
    BT102 .D37 2001
    231—dc21
                                                        00-049018

We hope you enjoy this book from Moody Publishers. Our goal is to provide
high-quality, thought-provoking books and products that connect truth to your
real needs and challenges. For more information on other books and products
written and produced from a biblical perspective, go to www.moodypublish-
ers.com or write to:

Moody Publishers
820 N. LaSalle Boulevard
Chicago, IL 60610

3 5 7 9 10 8 6 4

Printed in the United States of America

CONTENTS

FOREWORD

Prayer, meditation, and temptation (in the sense of being pressed hard and having to fight back) are the three things that make a theologian, said Luther. By that standard Dan DeHaan clearly qualified.

With his high-speed mind and ardent heart, Dan was a man whose vision, life, and message matched Oswald Chambers's great phrase—"My utmost for His Highest." And Chambers would have hailed him as a kindred spirit for showing as he did that the Father-child relation is central in Christianity, that there is gaiety in godliness, and that the reason godliness matters so much is that God matters more.

What Dan has written has high protein content for Christian people, though it must be read prayerfully and slowly if it is to have its full energizing effect. I invite you to do just that, and get the benefit.

J. I. PACKER

PREFACE

Several months ago I was teaching Colossians in the Metro Bible Study in Atlanta. Many people came to me after class and asked questions. Some were answered easily, whereas others were quite difficult. But as time went on I discovered a common weakness among the Christians of today. They were weak in their understanding of God and His character. Their questions concerning various topics such as knowing God's will, assurance of salvation, home life, and even dating relationships resulted from a definite lack in comprehending the person of God the Father. The burden in my heart grew heavier as I continued to teach. The more deeply involved I became in my exposition, the greater I felt the need to communicate to them something about the perfections of God. Many of the truths in this book come from my desire that God the Father be put back into the Christian's perspective on what it means to live that way of life called Christianity.

1
GOD:
I WANT
TO KNOW YOU!

How would you answer the question, Where does personal Christianity begin? The average Christian would say that it begins with accepting Christ as Savior and Lord. That is not true according to the Bible. Personal Christianity begins with the existence of an objective and infinite God.

Genesis 1:1 assumes God; it does not debate His existence. If that personal and infinite God is not the starting point of creation, then we are left to explain every area of life according to frail and questionable speculations. Christians believe in one big, bold miracle—God. As a result, everything else fits into place. The rest of the world denies God, the Creator, and needs a miracle to explain everything created.

If I were truly perfect in all of my ways—in my love, motives, actions, and attitudes, and I had the power to create whatever I wanted, would I not create a being who could appreciate me for what I am? If I were that kind of person and I knew how to transfer that perfection to you, would I not spend my energies doing so? The answer is obvious. God knew His power and perfection and longed to create men to appreciate Him. God created men to know Him. God created men to enjoy Him. God put in men's hearts the "God-shaped vacuum" that could only be filled with Himself. Personal Christianity begins with that infinite God. Only His person can satisfy man's cry for reality.

No other earthly creation can appreciate God for who He is. Only people have the capacity to glorify God on every level of His revealed character. God longed to create a man with whom He could commune. When we begin to see that as the starting point in personal Christianity, we then see that we are involved in something much bigger than just getting people to "commit their lives to Christ."

We must know God before we can do His will.

Does God have something to say about Himself that makes our commitment to Christ all the more enjoyable and real? The resounding answer is "Yes!" Could Christ's death on the cross mean much at all apart from God's prior revelation of Himself? The resounding answer is "No!" Present-day tendencies to talk of Jesus to the point of leaving out God the Father give a cult approach to God the Son. The way many talk of Christ's death, burial, and resurrection, it is as though those events constituted an end in themselves. Yes, they are central in the heart of God, but they only have substance in relation to God's prior revelation of Himself to man.

"And this is eternal life, that they may know Thee" (John

17:3). According to that verse, the Christian life is qualitative life, not merely quantitative. It is *presently eternal life*—to know God. Why did God create us? To fellowship with us. Why did Christ come to earth? To restore broken fellowship.

Let me warn you here, we must know God before we can do His will. God's character is at stake in our service to Him. Many of us have belittled the name of God to the point that He exists to meet needs, becoming nothing more than a spiritual Santa Claus. We live as if there were not much to God apart from meeting our needs. If there is more to God than that, we have given up the drive to press on to know Him. In most places I preach, people know little of the desire and motivation God gives through pressing on to know Him. They have had "sermonettes for Christianettes" and wonder why they cannot spend a day alone with God and enjoy it thoroughly.

First John 2 gives us the three stages of maturity among believers. John speaks of the *"little child"* as the one who understands that his sins are forgiven. That stage is very important and in understanding it, we all say "Amen." The *"young men"* are those who have overcome the wicked one. At that point we have a great drop-out rate among our ranks. There are those strong enough to take on spiritual warfare without hurting God's name in the process, but they are fewer and fewer compared to what we have seen in church history. Finally, John says the third category is *"fathers."* They are such because they "know God." It is important to note that "fathers" are referred to not only because they are older, but also because it is the father that produces children. They are selfless and secure enough to "grow others up." God knows we are in great need of a double dose of "fathers" within Christianity, not men who are supersaints, but men who understand and know God. That alone will give direction to the sleeping giant called the "church."

THE SIN OF IDOLATRY

The Bible speaks often about the sin of idolatry. Today, when people think of idolatry, they think of it in terms of worshiping a heathen god or a wooden image. The Bible calls idolatry any form of thinking about God wrongfully. The great need of the hour is twofold: first, the church must understand God as He is revealed to us; second, the church must be made secure in knowing Him.

Paul was one man who knew God. When Paul was in his middle sixties near death, he wrote to Timothy that in the last days men shall be "lovers of self . . . lovers of pleasure rather than lovers of God" (2 Timothy 3:2–5). He could easily be speaking of the church today when he goes on to say that many will hold "to a form of godliness" but deny its power. In effect, Paul is telling us that men will have performance without any passion. They will have a ministry without any motivation—divine motivation. That theme is continued in one of the last messages to the church.

The second chapter of Revelation tells of the church at Ephesus. Their performance was in line, but their motivation was gone. They were more acquainted with having a "handle" on their ministry than having a "handle" on God Himself. They had beautiful form but had no favor with God. "I know your deeds and your toil and perseverance . . . and you . . . have endured for My name's sake. . . . But I have this against you, that you have left your first love" (Revelation 2:2–4).

It is obvious that God desires our love. We cannot have intimate fellowship with one we do not love, and we cannot love one we do not know; therefore, we must pass on to know Him. The level of *love* for Him is directly related to our desire to seek Him. The word love is the pivotal word in the Bible. Whatever or whomever we love will motivate us. The greater our knowledge of God, the greater will be our love for Him, and likewise the greater our love for God, the greater our motivation. If we do not seek and find our love in God Himself, we will seek it elsewhere. That takes place among many today. It marks the beginning of worshiping the transient and the temporal. The result is a life in which there is little stability, security, and understanding in doing God's will.

In Luke 18 our Lord gave a parable for the last days. In verse 1 He tells us clearly that men "ought to pray and not to lose heart." In verse 8 He continues, asking certain questions. Will the Son of man find faith on the earth in those last days? He asks the question as though He was expecting "No" for an answer. Hear what He says. Will there be people so secure in the "last days" that they will neither give up nor mar God's name through that difficult day? That kind of security would have to be the type God alone can give, that which is lodged in the center of His character and revealed person. Scripture emphasizes the idea that we must find our security in God before we seek it in an activity for God. Many today find their joy and security in what they do for God rather than in what they are to God.

It is the vertical relationship between God and man that is to give expression to the horizontal plane of ministry. This is clear throughout the Word of God (John 21:15–17; James 2:1, 9, 12–13; 1 Peter 1:22). When we make our ministry or service on the horizontal plane the gauge as to how we are doing spiritually, we tend to look at our gift of natural energy as what God desires, rather than His anointing on a life.

Occasionally, I will meet someone who really wants to know God. One evening after the message I was counseling in my office. Seven or eight people were lined up to speak to me. One by one they asked questions to see if I could make the message clearer. Finally, a seventeen-year-old boy came. He had waited until the rest had gone. He ran to me and buried his head in his hands and cried. Thinking there was a big problem on his mind, I geared myself to meet it.

The young man asked, "Dan, do you ever get tired of hearing people ask you the same old questions that they could just as well get answers for from someone else?"

"Sometimes, I do," I replied.

He said, "I am here because I long to know God. I have been listening to you week after week, and God has made me so desperately hungry to know Him as you do. Does anyone ever come to you with this desire?"

I was stunned, realizing that this boy was rare. I had counseled fifty people before him who were not interested in knowing God more. As we prayed and committed our lives to one another, God increased the burden for the two of us to keep each other sharp spiritually. I have many friends, but those closest to me motivate my thirst after God.

God delights in nothing more than revealing Himself to His creatures.

It is important here that you understand the difference between "knowing" someone and really *knowing* someone. Paul spoke in Philippians of having the goal of *knowing* the Lord. I can assure you he already knew the Lord when he wrote the statement. He had been a Christian for thirty years. What could he have meant? Paul was aware that there was a higher plane of knowing the Lord, just as a husband

and wife can know one another after thirty years of marriage. Paul was not speaking of a casual acquaintance or an "easy come, easy go" relationship. With passion Paul pressed on to know God—and he knew God. Can we do less? Dare we do less? There is no other explanation for Paul's great, continued motivation and security in God's service than the fact that God honored Paul's pressing goal to know Him.

"I want to know God!" was the cry of this man. He was already strong in the Lord. I know what he meant. My heart burst in tears also as I identified with his plea. He wanted to *know* God. There is nothing that God would rather see in His created children. We were made for that purpose. We are striking the very core of divine desire. The very fact that we are content in our walk with God and are not moved to press on to *know* Him is a sad commentary on our day. God must raise up greater discontent on this issue. If He does not, the last days will find "no faith on the earth." Self-motivation and self-security will abound and, along with that, disappointment, discouragement, depression, and despair.

When we realize that God delights in nothing more than revealing Himself to His creatures, then we understand why *knowing* Him is our highest calling. In fact, we are allowed to brag about nothing else except that we know God. "'Let not a wise man boast of his wisdom, and let not the mighty man boast of his might, let not a rich man boast of his riches; but let him who boasts boast of this, *that he understands and knows Me,* that I am the Lord who exercises lovingkindness, justice, and righteousness on earth; *for I delight in these things,*' declares the Lord" (Jeremiah 9:23–24, italics added).

Many Christians are tired of serving the Lord simply for some reward they will receive in the "by and by." They find themselves living for the Lord out of *duty* and not out of *devotion.* They think, "If I just do right, then I will be right." The Bible makes clear that it is not what you "do" that

counts with God; it is what you "be" that is important. It is
character over conduct. As we get to *know* God, His character rubs off on us, and our conduct becomes purely an extension of what we know. "For I delight in loyalty rather
than sacrifice, and in the *knowledge of God rather than burnt
offerings*" (Hosea 6:6, italics added). We have been told for
so long to "stand up for Jesus." However, we must first learn
to "sit down with Jesus." Our standing is merely a tempo-
rary exercise if we have not learned how to sit at His feet.

THE RESULTS OF KNOWING GOD

There are ten great by-products of *knowing* God. If we
need biblical results for such an exercise, we are not left
empty-handed.

Character development. "Set your mind *on the things
above*, not on the things that are on earth. . . . Consider the
members of your earthly body as dead to [lusts]" (Colossians 3:2, 5, italics added). In counseling I deal with an un-
usual amount of people who battle over the issue, "How do
I discipline my mind?" I tell them, "Whatever you think,
you will become!"

Mind-preoccupation will determine our goals, our enjoyment of reality, and our ability to affect other people's
lives for the better. In order for Christlike behavior to be a
way of life, there must be a preoccupation with "things
above." That is not a dreamy kind of thing. It is the conscious worship of God's character that conforms us to what
we worship. We always become what we worship. That is a
law within even earthly relationships. What you bow down
before, you become enamored with. Some people ponder
and brood over their past victories or failures. They become
past-conscious. Their day begins with the past. As a result,
they can never really be what they should be right now, for

this moment. Other people are preoccupied with position, possessions, or pleasure. They actually worship those things. Whether they know it or not, those are the things that control their thoughts throughout the day. They are becoming what they worship.

Obviously, if we choose to worship that which is passing away, we reap the fruit of an equally unstable mind and character. Find me a worshiper of God, and I will show you a stable man with his mind in control, ready to meet the present hour with refreshment from above. Because the average person spends much of his time in either reading or watching someone else perform, it follows that his life is a by-product of what he has seen the most.

What things is your mind set on the most? You must answer that question. It will determine your entire character. God tells us that character can be transformed; it is not just left for events to control. "Where your treasure is, there will *your heart be also*" (Matthew 6:21, italics added). Romans 12:1–2 tells us that true worship transforms the mind. Colossians 2:2–3 tells us that true knowledge of God will produce wisdom and knowledge. That is quite a guarantee. It implies transformed mind and character. Paul put it this way: Gaze on Him and be "transformed" (2 Corinthians 3:18). Learning to worship is the key to mind control and character development.

I require my children to spend an hour alone every day. I do not dictate what they do during that hour. I encourage their quietness for at least an hour because of what it does to their minds and spirits. The result of that quietness can be seen in the children's love for one another and in their lack of murmuring. Don't misunderstand. What I am talking about is the spirit of my children being quiet and sensitive to others. We still laugh loudly and play with gusto, but the inner man of each of them is at home with God. My children's ages range from six to nineteen. If this can happen in them, it can happen to all of us. Is your life characterized by an inner spirit of quietness and strength? If not, check what or whom you are worshiping. Gaze on Him and be transformed.

Freedom from intimidation. Many Christians live according to the Christianity of other individuals. They walk a tightrope that others have erected for them. They seem to be doing fine until some "supersaint" comes and convinces them they are all wrong. The apostle Paul knew of that danger. He tells us in Philippians to beware of the "concision," that is, the false legalist. Paul says that kind of person is out to ruin our joy in the Lord. Colossians, chapter 2, is devoted to getting our minds stable in God in order to combat "superspiritual" intimidation.

Paul mentions four classes of people who try to intimidate us: philosophers, legalists, ascetics, and mystics. The philosophers tell us that we need more knowledge to be what God wants us to be. They make us feel like mental midgets in our walk with God. The legalists try to convict us for not adhering to their lists of dos and don'ts. The ascetics tell us that we have not given up enough yet. Only then, they say, will we be what God wants. Last, the mystics tell us that our experience has not been deep enough to be truly spiritual. One of the greatest satanic lies today is that even though you are a Christian, you still do not have it all. The Lord alone causes growth in our lives. He is our "pituitary gland."

Paul tells us in Colossians 2:23 what to think of manmade regulations that come across as having wisdom but draw us away from the centrality of Christ. He says they are self-imposed, indulge the flesh, and are of no value whatsoever. Those are harsh words for the intimidators. We are to have and to preach convictions, but we are not to give peo-

God: I Want to Know You!

ple the impression that the convictions make them holy. Holiness is the outgrowth of the worship of the Godhead. Keep your eyes on Christ and let Him feed you as you remain in His Word. Anyone who tries to draw a sharp contrast between yourself and himself is disguising pride with false humility. Get to know God so that your convictions are your own. The early Christians took for granted that holiness was expected among believers. There was no debate on that issue, because they knew and worshiped God. They did not have strict standards because someone preached that they should, but rather God's holiness rubbed off on them through their worship of Him.

Passion for the lost person. Many people battle with trying to work up a desire to win lost men and women to Christ. They need to understand that that desire is given to us in direct proportion to the communion we have with God. Someone has said, "Earthbound saints offer little to hellbound sinners." If we are not living where Christ is seated, and if our minds are not knowing His thoughts, we will approach a needy world with a heart of apathy. The key to missions is the key to the prayer closet—spending time alone with God.

We cannot work up what God alone can give. Isaiah 6 says that as the Lord is seen clearly in worship, we will have a proper view of our world around us. Isaiah's experience is the example of that. Having seen the Lord in His fullness and holiness, he saw himself and his world as unclean. After being cleansed in the presence of God, he cried out, "*Send me!*" (v. 8). In a day when most are saying, "Send someone else," we know we are in need of worshipers. Our selfishness has overruled our motivation; we carry no burden that makes us ache for men outside of Christ.

Energy in serving the Lord. "But the people who know their God will display *strength and take action*" (Daniel

21

11:32*b*, italics added). It is the worship and knowledge of God that gives energy to serve Him. The missing ingredient in the diet of the church today is worship. It is the cause for many anemic saints. They know what they should do but have little energy to do it. The early church was a worshiping church. Notice the energy they had in Acts 1 to 6.

Hudson Taylor lived so much in the presence of Jesus Christ that he began to feel the burden of Jesus for lost souls. He said that the burden of Christ became his burden. He found the self-satisfied church in England intolerable. The atmosphere of smug piety sickened him. The security of Christians was found in their possessions, not in their heavenly prize. Staggering out alone, he prayed for twenty-four men to go with him to China, and then he left. Why did no one else have such energy? Others' energies were all taken up with their worship of their possessions, their plans, and their performances before men.

A young Alpine climber prepares to ascend the Alps. Into his pack go the necessities he thinks are important for the trip. His load becomes quite heavy. Early in the climb he is physically exhausted. His body is wearied through its excessive burden. Finally, his guide tells him a choice must be made because not only is he hindering his own progress but also that of the other climbers to whom he is roped. He must either give up his hope of reaching the summit or cast aside the weight. Does he covet the prize enough to count all those things but loss that he may gain the Alpine summit? Spiritually, whatever our hindrance is in reaching the summit, it must be removed. Our spiritual resistance will be lowered if we choose not to let go of the weights and hindrances to worshiping and knowing God.

Renewed thoughts of God. Today's "easy believism" doctrine tells us that God is more of a kind gentleman than One who has authority. The value of thinking properly about

God is seen in how we talk and pray. We will always act according to how we think. "As [a man] thinks within himself, so he is" (Proverbs 23:7). Before we see God bring about a change in this generation, we must change our thinking about God and His character.

True satisfaction in God. I love the apostle Paul for what he has taught me on this level. He had such contentment in situations, no matter what they were like. He had joy in jail, he rejoiced in rivalry, he had contentment in conflict, and even delight in death. He knew what true worship was. Paul always viewed himself as "in Christ," not "in jail." His thoughts were elevated far beyond the circumstances of the mundane. He taught that the world cannot satisfy. Its difficulties do not have to shake us. God is calling out a people today to live as Paul did, whose lives convey the view that ultimate satisfaction can result only from knowledge of God.

Boldness for God. Again, the early church had boldness in right order. When they met to adore, admire, and become fascinated with the Almighty, they left with great boldness. They would say as Paul had said, "To live is Christ, and to die is gain" (Philippians 1:21). What he was saying was, "You can kill me—that will be gain, or you can let me live—that will be Christ. Both ways I win, you lose!" Do you have that boldness? It is not just for evangelical extroverts. It is for those who worship.

Worship keeps us from putting Christianity into compartments. The reason for today's division between the secular and the sacred in the minds of Christians is lack of individuals who worship and know God. The God of the Bible was involved in every area of the life of His children: what they ate, their bodily exercise, their rest, their festivals, and their worship. Today we assume God is good only for spiritual things. Our minds have pushed Him into having effect in a few areas only. He has much to say about church but offers little insight and enthusiasm to the mundane areas of the secular. How tragic—especially for our youth! I do not even like to use the question, "Is Christ first in your heart?" It gives the idea that something else is second or third. He must be central and work from that position to every compartment in our lives. As we worship Him, we find insight into how to make Him as real on the basketball court as in our church service.

The cure for situational ethics. I suppose that many would think that is not a problem among Christians. However, the philosophies of this day have run long enough to make situationalism a problem to the mind that is not anchored soundly. The individual who adheres to situational ethics says that all rules have exceptions, and that the Ten Commandments may be rightly overridden if in doing so you can do more people more good. That makes every situation a question as to whether law keeping is the best we can do. Even moral life becomes like a structureless musical composition in which one improvises rather than plays the notes on the score. The person who follows situational ethics justifies all kinds of deeds on the basis that it was done for a good cause. The church is not free to have "jam sessions" on clear issues. God's character is revealed as the ultimate standard in every debate we would entertain. The end never justifies the means. Present-day America is suffering severely from reaping what it has sown as a result of situational ethics.

Knowing the difference between repentance and remorse. Paul made the clear distinction in 2 Corinthians 7:9–11. Remorse is sorrow in which man is truly sorry for what he did, but he never sees it as God sees it. The remorseful man sees the consequences of wrongdoing and mourns over that. Both Cain in the Old Testament and Judas in the New Testament are illustrations of that. To repent of something one must know God enough to know how He feels about the sin.

There is more questioning today about the need for repentance than ever before. Our lack of knowing God's character is the reason. When David repented of his sin in Psalm 51, he immediately related it to God's character. Repentance is impossible unless we see sin as God sees it. We do not need someone else's opinion of our sins; we need God's. To repent means to come to the cross and leave the sin there, after we have already seen it for what it was before God. That is why in all true repentance that leads to salvation there is a deep humbling of the life.

One cannot stand erect spiritually and see one's sin as God sees it. It has to break the heart. Has yours been broken? Does God's character not shed any light on the wrongness of sin? A man who worships God becomes a man who keeps "short accounts" with God. Sin is seen for what it is.

We have seen ten clear by-products of knowing God and worshiping Him. Can you say that those ten areas are clearly lived in your life? In which areas are you weak? The cure is in understanding and knowing God. As you continue through this book, pray that God would open your eyes to all that He is.

Prayer: O God, is it true that I can be a worshiper of You? I open myself up for You to do just that. Let me know You that I may know Your anointing on my life. I pray as I continue in this book that You would not let me miss anything that You have for me. I give myself to You right now. I will be still and know that You are God. In knowing You, I will love You, and in loving You, I will serve You. In Jesus' name I pray. Amen.

2
THE
GLORY
OF GOD

As a boy I had the thrill of seeing a total eclipse of the moon. I remember sitting out in the front yard and watching the moon getting darker and darker. The earth was between the moon and the sun and, therefore, the earth's shadow was cast upon the moon.

The glory of God may be likened to the sun. I realize that the sun is only a created "ambassador" of God's full glory, but it does serve to illustrate God's brightness. Today we hear very little of the glory of God. I do not know that I have heard more than three sermons on the topic. As the moon is eclipsed by the earth, the saints are being eclipsed through allowing other people or things to stand between them and God's glory. The result is tragic for both man and God. Man has no sunshine in his life, and God does not get the glory He deserves.

GOD'S ATTRIBUTES

God's glory is the total manifestation of all His attributes. His glory is what will make heaven what it will be. There will be no hindrance to God's brightness and no shadow cast upon God's glory because of sin. People have asked me how eternal life can last forever. We have the answer to that question when we understand God's glory, which is so unsearchable that it will take all eternity to begin to discover. On earth we know of certain attributes of God, but they constitute only a small part of God's nature. Their function is to relate God's character to us while we are here on earth. Imagine what He is saving for us to discover throughout all eternity. Understanding His glory will become a never-ending adventure.

The Bible begins and ends with God's glory.

Suppose you go fishing at a quiet little pond. As you fish you spend about ten minutes at each spot. After two hours you have fished the entire circumference of the pond, or at least you thought you had. As you near the end, you see an outflow of the pond. Looking up in amazement, you see the ocean. All of a sudden you are involved with something that is unsearchable. You laugh over how small you feel in comparison. That little pond was just a small extension of the ocean. That is what God's glory is like. It is unsearchable.

God's glory is certainly shaded here on earth. Sin has made man think that he can steal part of God's glory. Men down through history have laughed at God only to find that their misery increased as a result. God will get His glory. It will not be shared with anyone. Men can laugh God out of schools, out of books, and even out of their lives, but man cannot laugh Him out of his death. Voltaire, the French infidel who tried to demolish Christianity and turn out the lights on God's glory, sang a different tune on his deathbed. Speaking to his doctor he said, "I will give you half of what I am worth, if you will give me six months more to live. Then I shall go to hell, and you will go with me." Voltaire tried to do what he could never do: to rob God's glory.

The Bible begins and ends with God's glory. In Genesis we see His glory in creation. It is still true according to Psalm 19 that "the heavens *declare the glory of God*" (v. 1, KJV, italics added). Any study of the universe, no matter how small the approach, will bring a person to glorify God in some way. God has made it that way. Man can study hydrology, astronomy, meteorology, geology, or even physiology and still find the amazing creative energy of God. God's creation is the greatest visible display of His glory. It is a foretaste on earth of what will come later.

One can illustrate that glory through the star called "Betelgeuse." It is a distant star next to Orion. It happens to be 527 light-years away from the earth. Light traveling at a speed of 186,000 miles a second still takes 527 light-years to reach the earth. What is amazing about Betelgeuse is its size. It is twice the size of the earth's orbit around the sun. What kind of creative energy created that star? When we realize that nothing created is as great or complex as the one who created it, that gives us a small idea of the *glory* of God.

GOD'S CREATION

Nowhere in the Bible does God try to prove His existence. But, have you ever considered how much more difficult it is to disprove God's existence? Napoleon, while standing one night on the deck of a ship, was asked, "Is there a God?" On hearing the question, he raised his hand and, pointing to the starry firmament, simply responded, "Gentlemen, who made all that?"

The sun can be used to illustrate God's glory most vividly.

Though the sun is the source and fountain of light, there is little good in gazing at the sun, unless one desires to be blinded. No one ever had his sight improved as the result of looking directly at the sun. We use the sun's light to search things out, but there is no searching of the sun itself; our eyes are too weak. How much less can we search out the sun's Creator, before whom the multitudes of suns are like the grains of sand in the desert.

It must grieve the Lord to see all of His creation glorifying Him, except man. Stars shine, and in doing so, they glorify God. They were created to do so. There is no revolt among the stars out of boredom or rebellion. There is never a blackout in the heavens. Animals also do as they were created to do. Only man and angels revolt, trying to glorify themselves instead of their Creator.

The first two commandments in Exodus 20 reveal God's concern that man give Him glory. The first commandment is to have "no other gods before Me." The second is "You shall not make . . . an idol" (vv. 3–4). Both of those have to do directly with God's glory. He protects it first. Why are we not to worship other gods? Because we will begin to think of God Himself in terms of the other gods we worship. Why are we not to make graven images? Because we will be tempted to think of God in terms of them. Every time we make an image it causes something to be lost in our concept of God's character of glory. Aaron's golden calf demonstrated the might of God, but it missed His moral character, His goodness, righteousness, and patience. A crucifix obscures His glory by concealing His deity, His victory, and strength. All images mislead men into thinking erroneously about God.

 What God longs to teach us is that when we have nothing left but God, God is enough. We find ourselves chasing so many different things. But when God's glory is known and truly desired, we will settle for nothing less. At Christ's birth the angels said, "Glory to God in the highest." That will be the motto of heaven for all eternity.

When a person is hurt through the loss of someone close to him, he sometimes strikes out at God and tries to deny His power. The danger in that is clear; we are too ignorant to judge God for what appears to be a failure. A pastor visited a family whose son had been killed in an automobile accident. He heard the mother lash out at him, "Where was your God when my boy was killed?" He quietly responded, "The same place He was when His Son was killed."

We emphasize what God does for us, rather than who He is in Himself.

If we were to take a stick and put it into a glass of water, it would seem to be crooked. Why? Because we look at it through two mediums—air and water. It is the same with our understanding of God. His various characteristics, such as His justice, seem crooked to us. The wicked seem to prosper and the righteous suffer. It seems that unfair events take place all the time. The problem is not with God but with us. We view God's proceedings through a double medium of flesh and spirit. Therefore, it is not that God's character is bent, it is that man is not competent to judge.

In the study of the sciences man stands above the object of investigation. But that is not the case with God, who says of Himself that His ways are past finding out (Romans 11:33–34). In theology, man is under the One he is investigating; therefore, God must reveal Himself before man can investigate further. Man is on the defensive, and he does not like that role. We want to control what we investigate. That cannot be done with God. That is why we are allowed to brag about knowing God according to Jeremiah 9:23–24. In knowing God, it took His revealing Himself to us, as opposed to our discovering Him. Blessed is the man who has had God visit him. All other bragging is self-centered because man did something or discovered something through his own investigation.

God alone is to be glorified. The very first words of the Westminster Catechism hit at the core of that point. What is the chief end of man? "The chief end of man is to glorify God and to enjoy Him forever." Everything God made was for His glory (Colossians 1:16). No person understanding the reason for his being created would seek to shadow God's glory. God tells us He will not share His glory with any other (Isaiah 42:8). All things are to be done for His glory (1 Corinthians 10:31).

It is against the backdrop of the revelation of God's glory that rebellion against God becomes senseless. People challenge God and think they are winning. Incredible! Pride has to be a form of insanity. How could created beings climb on the throne of God's glory? Even our form of "lightbulb" evangelism today denies much of God's glory. It is bright for a moment, but it soon fades away. Why does it fade? Because we emphasize what God does for us, rather than who He is in Himself. Often people come to Christ with selfish motives, but we were created and re-created for God's pleasure and glory. Only as that is fulfilled in us does our enjoyment in God thrive.

Seeing that every creation does what it is created to do with the exception of man makes God's dealings with man all the more significant. Why are we so special that God would take so much care and bother to share Himself with man? Who can explain the enduring patience and mercy of God in His efforts to restore man to His glory? First Peter 3:19–20 tells us that the angels were doomed after revolting against God. Why not man? The answer to that sheds incredible light on God's glorious character. To understand it we must see God's great attempts in presenting Himself to his special creation—man.

The third chapter of Genesis gives the first visible glimpse of the glory of God. God introduces the devil in the early verses as one who deceives, fosters pride, and brings into bondage. After the fall of man we come to verse 8, "And they heard the sound of the Lord God walking in the garden . . . , and the man and his wife hid themselves from the *presence* of the Lord God . . ." (italics added).

That *presence* of God could be illustrated by the sun. The sun that grows wheat to feed millions can blind the person looking at it. Like the sun, His glory can supply or it can destroy. Like the sun, God projects—His beauty, His wooing, His entreating. Like the sun, He can do that everywhere at once (Habakkuk 3:4). In the Garden of Eden, His presence may have been the blazing, visible glory of God.

After man's fall, his image was marred. His rebellion resulted in his great delight in God's glory's turning to fear. For the first time salvation by works was introduced as they covered themselves with fig leaves. They tried to do something "in the flesh" to make themselves acceptable to God. For the first time they were fearful of their gracious God and were deceitful to one another. They "passed the buck," trying not to take the full blame for their sin. The very curse God put on them and the creation was prophetic of what He would later put on His Son.

What did Adam and Eve do with God's glory? They rejected it. God said, "Will you glorify Me?" Man said, "No." Genesis 3:22–23 tells us that man was dismissed from God's presence because he rejected God's glory. God drove man out of the Garden. He placed at the east of the Garden a flaming sword, which turned every way to keep them out

(Genesis 3:24). That flaming sword was a magnificent emblem of God's glorious justice and hatred for sin. Notice that sword turned every way to keep the entrance blocked. If it had not turned every way, if it had left some footpath uncovered, then Adam might have stolen in by that footpath and made his own way to the Tree of Life. Whatever avenue he tried, however secret, however narrow, however difficult, however silently he crept along, "still this flaming meteor met him, and it seemed to say 'How can men be just with God? By the deeds of the law there shall be no flesh living justified.' Well might Adam sit down, wearied with the vain search for a pathway into life; for man by nature has no way to the Father."[1]

But God did not give up on man, nor did He cast doom on him as He did on the angels. The story continues as we see God's persistence in revealing His glory to man. Exodus sheds the next ray of light on the topic. Certainly the burning bush was an illustration of God's glory, but in Exodus 33 we have a clearer definition. In verse 12 Moses is speaking and is a bit upset with God for giving him such a divine responsibility with so little help. "But Thou Thyself hast not let me know whom Thou wilt send with me." In other words, "Lord, You don't expect me to do this leading of three million people alone, do You?" I am sure he was thinking of how difficult it was to get his family packed for even a small trip.

Moses went on to pray in verse 13, "Now therefore, I pray Thee, if I have found favor in Thy sight, let me know Thy ways, that I may know Thee." Then the Lord answered and said to Moses, "My *presence* shall go with you, and I will give you rest" (v. 14, italics added). That is the same word for presence as in Genesis 3:8. Moses misunderstood what that presence was. After God told him it was His glory then Moses prayed this mighty request, *"I pray Thee, show me Thy glory!"* (v. 18).

God answered his desperate cry. Among the Parthians there was a custom that no parents were to give their children meat in the morning before they saw the sweat on their faces. That is God's usual plan, as well—not to give His children the taste of His delights until they begin to sweat in seeking them. Moses was sweating after God's glory, and he found it. God told him, "While My glory is passing by . . . I will put you in the cleft of the rock and cover you with My hand until I have passed by" (Exodus 33:22). Moses could not receive God's full glory and live (v. 20). It would have killed him! Imagine standing a few yards away from the sun. That would be a very small example of God's glory in its fullness. God's back passed by Moses while his face was hidden. Exodus 34 tells us what happened to Moses. His face shown like a lightbulb (v. 29). It so shone that Aaron and the others were afraid to come near him. Moses had to put a veil over his face to talk to the people.

God's desire to meet man is constant.

Paul comments in 2 Corinthians 3:13 on why Moses kept putting the veil over his face. Moses did not want the people to see the glory fading. Can you picture that sight? There was Moses, filled with God's glory, carrying that glory to the people. How did they respond to it? They rejected it! They said, "We want no part of this God or His glory." But did God give up? No.

Today we must do the same thing that Moses did. Those of us who are leaders must carry God's presence into the lives of people. Most of us do the opposite. We carry people into the presence of God. We must come down from His presence to minister with anointing from above. If people trample on the glory of God, that should not drive us away from returning to the place of blessing to receive further from God's glory. We are to be men and women bent on the glory of God. It should consume us as it did Moses. Our perseverance in bringing God's glory to the people will ultimately bring lasting results.

Exodus 40:34 brings more insight into God's drive to communicate His glory to us. The tabernacle was a tent made of an ugly skin that would blacken as it weathered. The only thing beautiful about it was the inside. God's glory filled the entire tent. It housed God's glory. Why you ask, was the tabernacle needed among God's people? God had to have a place for men to meet with Him. God's desire to meet man is constant. When man's desire matches God's, there is an explosion of reality in God's glory. Moses was unable even to enter the tent, because the manifestation of God's glory was too strong (v. 35). Imagine such a thing—God's glory in the middle of the desert among the twelve tribes. His glory was for everyone to behold. Did they acknowledge God through it? No. They complained and murmured and desired to be back under the slavery of wicked men rather than be in the presence of God. What amazing persistence on the part of God and what amazing rebellion from men!

At times, like Moses, I want to tell God to stop and share no more with this people. My patience is through, but His continues on. They do not deserve it. Then I realize that I am part of that crowd—I do not deserve it either. My heart cries out, "Lord, show me more. Don't stop now. Press on to reveal Yourself to me."

Is that your cry? I agree with David Brainerd when he said, "I saw more of the majesty and glory of God in these chapters of Exodus than ever I had seen before. Frequently, in the meantime, I fell on my knees and cried to God for the faith of Moses and for a manifestation of the divine glory."[2]

The next clear revealing of God's glory is found in First Kings 8:10. At that point the glory of God's presence appeared in the temple that Solomon built. Again God's glory was so strong the priests could not stand to minister (v. 11). Was there a resounding thrill of joy over that revelation of God? If there were, it was short-lived. The people continued to commit sins of idolatry and immorality. They would not recognize God's glory. When the queen of Sheba came to see the temple, she gave all the glory to Solomon for its wonder (2 Chronicles 9).

The prophet Ezekiel was the recorder of the last view of God's glory in the Old Testament. In chapters 8–10 we see the final sad account of God's attempt to communicate His glory. Those chapters record the results of rejecting God's glory. As the glory of God leaves, the abominations of wickedness increase. What a strong application for today's Christianity! As God's glory is rejected, there will be increased abominations. According to Ezekiel, those will take place in direct proportion to one another.

Ezekiel tells us that the entrance to the temple had become a place of idol worship (8:5). The people had the audacity to put an idol in place of God's glory—right in the lobby! And God was grieved. "Do you see what they are doing?" God said. "They are driving Me out from My own sanctuary. But yet you will see still greater abominations" (8:6).

Ezekiel 10 tells us the progressive way God's glory left the temple never to return. God's glory was gone! Surely God's patience was over for good. Men had rejected His presence. Men had rejected His man Moses. Men had rejected His Shekinah cloud of protection and guidance. Men rejected

His glory in the tabernacle. Men rejected His glory in the temple. They even replaced His glory with idols of their own making. Would God give up?

God, in a sense, began all over in the person of His Son, Jesus Christ. To confirm Christ's deity that He was truly God before becoming man, John records in 1:14, "And the Word became flesh, and dwelt among us, and we beheld His glory, glory as of the only begotten from the Father, full of grace and truth." Luke 9:29 speaks of the Mount of Transfiguration, where Jesus put His fleshly state aside and was transformed into His true glory. First John 1:1 tells us that they "handled" that glory of God in the person of Christ. Certainly, this time the world would respond. But "He came to His own, and those who were His own did not receive Him" (John 1:11).

Stephen before the Sanhedrin (Acts 7) spoke of the glory of God as it was revealed to Abraham. That glory caused Abraham to leave his country, his comforts, and his companions. Stephen told them that it was that glory that they were rejecting. Stephen was stoned for such a demonstration of God's heart through his message. "But being full of the Holy Spirit, he gazed intently into heaven and *saw the glory of God,* and Jesus standing at the right hand of God" (Acts 7:55, italics added). Twice Scripture says that Stephen saw Jesus standing. All other places in Scripture He is seated next to the Father. Why was He standing here? It seems that Stephen's response to God's glory moved God Himself to respond to Stephen with such honor. He stood to welcome the glory of God upon that one man.

Colossians 1:27 says, "Christ in you, [is] the hope of glory." Christ "in us" is the evidence that we have believed in Christ. Christ "in us" is the proof that we carry no glory of our own, only His glory that is imputed to us. That is fitness for glory! Heaven has already begun. The kingdom of God is within us.

We must make sure Christ lives in us. Have we put on Christ? Do we have a dream, or is there real hope—evidence? Are we fit for glory? Does Christ live in us and walk in us? "Without [holiness] no one will see the Lord" (Hebrews 12:14). We are now His Garden of Eden, His tent, His temple, His housing. "Do you not know that your body is a temple of the Holy Spirit who is in you?" (1 Corinthians 6:19).

Matthew 24:29 speaks of God's glory in the future: The sky will become dark in order to let God's glory have no competition whatsoever. We know that in heaven the only light will be the light of God flashing its way into eternity. Colossians 3:4 tells us that we will be there with Him in that day. It is His glory that will energize us to live forever.

Do you believe that God deserves glory? So many Christians live a subnormal life in terms of giving God glory. They are not happy in their rebellion. They just follow what their friends live, or they never consider pressing on to be more than a "Sunday believer." I trust you are ready to take the challenge to give God *total glory*.

The apostle Paul has given us some principles for handling questionable things in life. How can one know what is right and what is wrong when there are so many voices dictating today? Regarding any practice, we should be able to answer a question that Paul raises: "Can I do this for the glory of God?" If we cannot glorify God in what we are doing, we should not continue it. Quit making things difficult. Most areas are just that easy to discern if we are open to the Lord. There are neutral issues that neither give God glory nor take it away from Him—but we must be sure we can answer that question without our hearts' condemning us.

Another question to ask is, "Would Jesus do this if He were in my shoes?" That will not take care of everything, but it will answer many things. If we cannot picture Christ's doing it, we should not. Is "Christ in you, the hope of glory"?

What will it cost to arrange our lives to say yes to those questions? Is God's glory so special that we will pay the price, or is His glory "cheap," costing us very little? Until we allow God to put His finger on what is clearly not giving Him glory, we are in no position to expect Him to be strong on our behalf.

Jeremiah 13 gives us a sad yet profound look at God's concern in this area. It makes us wonder whether God is giving a commentary on our own generation. "Listen and give heed, do not be haughty, for the LORD has spoken. *Give glory to the Lord your God,* before He brings darkness and before your feet stumble on the dusky mountains, and while you are hoping for light He makes it into deep darkness, and turns it into gloom. But if you will not listen to it, *My soul will sob in secret for such pride; and my eyes will bitterly weep and flow down with tears*" (vv. 15–17, italics added).

Prayer: Lord, it is the cry of my heart to know You. I realize that it is Christ in me and my position in Christ that is the hope of glory. Teach me how to worship You so that I may carry Your glory into the presence of others. I give up my right to be preoccupied with the desires of this world. Show me Your glory! I desire to bring You such enjoyment that like Stephen, I would thrill You in life or death. Thank You for revealing Yourself to me. I do not deserve it, but I am truly grateful. To God be the glory! Amen.

NOTES

1. Andrew A. Bonar, *Memoirs of McCheyne* (Chicago: Moody, 1947), 163.

2. Jonathan Edwards, *The Life and Diary of David Brainerd* (Chicago: Moody, 1949), 140.

3

THE PERFECTIONS
OF GOD (PART 1)

I grew up in Michigan. It was there that I met the Lord one lonely evening in my home at the age of fourteen. I remember listening to great sermons in church when I was a boy and going away wondering what God wanted of my life. In the wintertime Lake Michigan would often freeze and I would spend Sunday afternoons out on that frozen ice. I would run out onto the lake, possibly half a mile, and sit all bundled up on a huge snowdrift that had been hardened from the wind. As I would sit there, I would contemplate what God was like.

I would ask questions out loud, often shouting them out. No one could hear except God. Alone with Him, I would ask, "Lord, would You make me like the saints of old? Lord, I want to be like the apostle Paul. How are You going to do that in me?" I would also ask Him about other things like, "Why is there such a large gap between Christians? Why are some committed, while others are not? Why do some love to talk of Your dealings with them and others could care less?" I would often cry out, "O God, don't let me join the ranks of the spiritual dropouts. Don't let me become careless and bored in my walk with You!" As I would spend hours at a time talking to God, I was able to see my desire transformed into determination.

Soon after my sixteenth birthday, a man told me to do a study on the character of God. Not knowing where to begin, I went to a Bible bookstore to read chapter after chapter from books on theology. Most of the time I did not even understand what was being said. It was not long before I discovered a book called *Systematic Theology,* by Louis Berkhof. It caused me to wrestle with some issues, and, as a result, that carried me out of a mundane Christian life. I found myself hungering to know God. I would carry my newfound knowledge out to the ice and "pray it through." I had more questions than answers, but I was willing to wait. As God would reveal Himself to me, I found His will more of a delight and His Word the enjoyment of my life. Psalm 40:8 became my favorite verse for some time. "I delight to do Thy will, O my God; Thy law is within my heart."

God's characteristics are nothing but perfect.

I say all of that to make this point: The deepest thought a person can ever have is his conception of God's character. As you begin to see how men like Abraham and Joseph grabbed hold of God for their needs and depended on Him, you begin to realize that you are no different from them. They knew God well and desired to know Him better.

Various individuals in Scripture possessed spiritual

qualities that were based on their knowing God. Try to understand the loneliness of Abraham and how he must have appreciated being called "the friend of God." Imagine the rugged discipline of Moses. Respect the unworldly heart of Joshua. Run to the bold stand of Daniel. Be silent before Deborah, that woman who knew God's strength well. In marking their "otherworldliness" learn of God's character and guidance through His servants. God will work in us also, as we get desperate in our desire to know His perfections.

This chapter is entitled "The Perfections of God." The reason for such a title is that all of God's attributes are perfect throughout. You may be impressed with God's wisdom, but it is perfect wisdom. You may be struck with God's justice, but again, it is perfect justice. That perfection is what makes it unlike our own. Men can have the same characteristics, but those characteristics are never perfect. God's characteristics are nothing but perfect. "Who is like Thee among the gods, O Lord? Who is like Thee, majestic in holiness, awesome in praises, working wonders?" (Exodus 15:11).

To many of us God is judged or praised by the "comparison method." For example, if we feel He loves us as we know love, then we praise Him. If we feel He acted wisely as we understand wisdom, then we exalt Him. We measure God by our own standards. When we are stumped as to why an event that is contrary to our liking and understanding took place, we immediately question God. God is infinite and perfect; man is finite and imperfect. Man, being a finite creature, uses his own mind and character as the criterion in determining whether God is worthy of praise or disparagement.

Some have read this far and are wondering why I have not questioned the existence of God for the sake of the agnostic. In my dealings with people, I do find a few honest

seekers who are agnostics, though not many. Among athe-
ists I find no honest seekers. The atheist, says Psalm 14:1, is
a fool. He is a fool because the only one he is "faking out" is
himself. Someone remains an atheist perhaps in order to believe he will not have to answer to a God who might require
punishment for sin. An atheist might say, "I can't find God
anywhere!" But an atheist cannot find God for the same reason that a thief cannot find a policeman. He is not truly interested in finding Him. Once the atheist is an agnostic
there is a basis for communication.

I am sure you have heard of the usual arguments against
atheism. One is the "cause and effect principle"—to have a
complex effect demands a complex cause. To believe that
the great complexity in this universe was created by no one
is a step based on empty faith. Another is the "law of intelligence or design." Intelligence comes from intelligence. A
design comes from a designer. If a watch could talk it would
confess the existence of a watchmaker. The watch did not
come together through an explosion in a watch factory. Order does not come out of chaos. I say all this to interject the
need to find those who are seeking after God and to be able
to respond to their questioning. The honest seeker is at least
open. Stay with him. The atheist is closed and is fighting
God on the inside of his life. His rebellion against God reveals that fight.

Charles Spurgeon said these words in one of his sermons:

> Many men believe in the existence of a God; but they do not
> love that belief. They know there is a God; but they greatly
> wish there were none. Some would be very pleased, yea,
> would set the bells a ringing, if you believed there were no
> God. Why, if there were no God, then you might live just as
> you liked; if there were no God, then you might run riot, and
> have no fear of future consequences. It would be to you the
> greatest joy that could be, if you heard that the eternal God

had ceased to be. But the Christian never wishes any such a thing as that. The thought that there is a God is the sunshine of his existence.[1]

The Bible speaks of God as incomprehensible.

What is God really like? Are we able to comprehend His perfections? The answers to those questions are found in the Word of God. The Bible does not answer the question, What is God? God has revealed Himself to us through His attributes. An attribute of God is simply anything that is true about Him, and we are left to God's revealing anything about Himself before we can know it. If God does not reveal, we cannot find. That is true in all of His ways. In Job 11:7, Job's friend Zophar asks, "Can you discover the depths of God? Can you discover the limits of the Almighty?" The force of that question demands the answer no. God is infinite; therefore, He must have an infinite number of attributes. We will spend all eternity searching out the unsearchableness of God. Isaac Watts conveys that thought in a hymn he wrote in 1707:

> Eternity, with all its years,
> Stands present in thy views;
> To thee there's nothing old appears;
> Great God, there's nothing new.

In *Systematic Theology* Berkhof writes, "The Bible never operates with an abstract concept of God, but always describes Him as the Living God, who enters into various relations with His creatures, relations which are indicative of several different attributes."[2] Therefore, we know God only so far as He enters into relations with us. Calvin speaks of those who believe they can comprehend God when he says, "They are merely toying with frigid speculations whose mind is set on the question of what God is, when what really concerns us to know is rather what kind of a person He is and what is appropriate to His nature."[3]

Our problem at this point is profound to say the least. We cannot think of God in terms of anything but the negative. When the Bible speaks of God as incomprehensible, it means just that—something we cannot comprehend (Psalm 145:3; Isaiah 40:28; Romans 11:33). Try right now as you read this to think of God's holiness. If you do, I will tell you what you are thinking. You are bound to think of the negative of holiness, that is, holiness is not sinning. Try right now to think of God's being limitless. You can only come to think of Him as not having limits. We only know limits. We only know what is measurable. God is not like any thing that we understand, because we can only understand what has boundaries and confinement. Try to think of eternity. C. S. Lewis suggests that we think of a sheet of paper infinitely extended. That would be eternity. Then on that paper draw a short line to represent time. As the line begins and ends on that infinite expanse, so time began in God and will end in Him.

No single book could contain the whole of God's character. It will take eternity to grasp it. Why then is it so mandatory for us to know God now? The reason is that man is made in God's image; therefore, no person can love God, serve God, be encouraged by God, or walk with God until he knows God. To the degree that we know Him will determine everything about us. God has made Himself knowable, but only in certain areas. His purpose in doing that was for our own good. When those few revelations of God's incomprehensible character are grasped, man's own character will begin to be altered. We are what we worship. It is God's life that we want, not human life trying to be godly.

It is interesting to note the men in Scripture whom God commissioned into His service only after giving them a bold revelation of Himself. Ezekiel tells us after his encounter with the character of God, "Such was the appearance of the likeness of the glory of the Lord. *And when I saw it, I fell on my face* and heard a voice speaking" (Ezekiel 1:28, italics added). In that same chapter Ezekiel had a revelation of who God is. He saw His majesty, His power, His holiness, His righteousness, His grace, even His skill and wisdom. The result was that Ezekiel fell on his face, humbled before God. The greatest problem of man—pride—is destroyed through contact with the revelation of God. That is why knowing a lot about the Word of God without knowing the God of the Word always produces pride.

God's glory blasts its way through the wall of pride. Every self-determined thought is melted, and the person sees himself as "undone" and in desperate need. When will teachers, preachers, and seminary students learn that apart from a clear revelation of God Himself, we had better not touch the ministry? If we have nothing of God's glory to take to the people, then the truth we speak only oppresses some or gives license to others. Yes, God's manifestation of Himself convicts, but only for the purpose of setting us free to be willing servants and children of such a great God and Father.

HIS IMMUTABILITY

Think of God's *immutability*—His unchanging nature. The Bible tells us that God changes not (Psalm 102:26–27; James 1:17). God speaking through Malachi said that He ought to destroy Israel, but He was not going to do so. He would not because, "I, the Lord, do not change" (Malachi 3:6). Charles Hodge states the unchanging character of God this way, "He can neither increase or decrease. He is subject to no process of development or of self-evolution. He can never be wiser or holier, or more righteous and merciful than He ever has been or will be."[4] Change can only take place for either the better or for the worse. God cannot get any better, and He certainly will not get worse. There is simply nothing to change.

The early church saw the unchanging character of God as represented by a cube. Place it any way; it will still be the same, because it is equal to itself in all dimensions. Others referred to Him as the center of a circle. The circumference may change; the center does not.

God is unchanging in His perfections, His purposes, and His promises. He is omniscient; He knows all things right now, and knows no more now than He did a thousand years ago. Hebrews 4:13 tells us that "all things are open and laid bare [naked] to the eyes of Him." One can say, "Well, I wonder if God saw what I was doing last weekend." Yes, He did. How convicting that is at times! Yet, how comforting it is to know that although everything else goes through change, God's purposes and promises stand sure. Whatever He plans He will do (Isaiah 46:11). His decrees are called mountains of bronze (Zechariah 6:1).

What does the attribute of God's immutability mean to the Christian? *Comfort.* Someone has a handle on this thing called life. Some things do not change. If ever God loved me, He loves me now. That is what unchangeable means. If ever God forgave me, He forgives me now. Someone reading this might say, "But I have committed a sin lately that is too bad." Stop and think! It is too bad in whose eyes? If God were like our fathers or mothers, then it might be too bad. If

God were like our employers or friends, then it might be too bad. God is not like them, because they change. He does not. God cannot deny Himself. If ever God promised me something, He promised me forever. I have had people tell me that they wished they could have lived during the time of the early church. According to them, God was different then. But God's promises have not changed. If ever God saved me, He saved me forever. "If we are faithless, He remains faithful; for He cannot deny Himself" (2 Timothy 2:13).

Our security in Scripture is based on God's absolute unchanging character. We say, "I cannot hang on," but our security is not based on any ability of ours to "hang on." We change. We have up days and down days. God does not change and He does not vacillate regarding His promises.

Stephen Charnock in his volume *The Existence and Attributes of God* says, "The line that is nearest to the place where it is first fixed, is least subject to motion; the further it is stretched from it, the weaker it is and more liable to be shaken."[5] What he is showing us is that we must *stay close to God* and humble ourselves before Him. To love Him we must know Him, and as we know Him our love will increase. As our love increases, we find that we obey the Lord unconsciously. What a thrill, to know and love someone so intimately that one finds oneself doing His will without even concentrating on it. God is looking for that kind of spontaneity and stability. Our only hope for that kind of life is to know Him.

What would God's unchanging character mean to an unbeliever? If God said that the wages of sin is death, He meant it. "Forever, O Lord, Thy Word is settled" (Psalm 119:89). If God said that there is an eternal hell, He meant it. All flesh must be silent before Him (Zechariah 2:13). His counsel shall stand and cannot be recalled. All struggling against it is like a brittle glass contending with a rock. Why must man be born again? He has to have God's unchanging principle of life put into him, for he is a dying creature.

HIS OMNIPOTENCE

Another perfection of God is His *omnipotence*. We cannot think of unrestrained power. We can think only in terms of what is measurable. God is all-powerful. People pray, "Lord, show us Thy power," but one could not see His unrestrained power and live. It is incomprehensible. A brief look at the book of Revelation will show us God's power unleashed on the heavens and earth. Everything is consumed. Today we see God's power in a very limited sense. He reveals His power only to the degree that the finite can handle the infinite.

"But our God is in the heavens; He does whatever He pleases" (Psalm 115:3). "Behold, Thou hast made the heavens and the earth by Thy great power and by Thine outstretched arm! Nothing is too difficult for Thee" (Jeremiah 32:17). Again, *what comfort!* There is a limit to everyone's ability but God's. *What conviction!* Psalm 1 says sinners shall not stand in the day of judgment. "Every knee shall bow." In the last days, men will try to put out God's power, and their attempts will be like shooting popguns at mountains. "Behold, I am the Lord, the God of all flesh; is anything too difficult for Me?" (Jeremiah 32:27).

HIS OMNISCIENCE

A third perfect attribute of God is His *omniscience*. A. W. Tozer observes, "To say that God is omniscient is to say that He possesses perfect knowledge and therefore has no need to learn. But it is more: it is to say that God has never learned and cannot learn."[6] Christians sometimes forget

God's omniscience when they pray, "Lord, I want to tell You about Sally's need." One little boy who was so excited over what happened at a meeting prayed, "Lord, it was so good. I can't thank You enough. Oh, Lord, it was so good. You just should have been there."

What does God's omniscience mean to the believer? It means that God never discovers anything; He is never surprised and never amazed. He never seeks out information. Only the infinite can know the infinite. That is why God said, "The thoughts of God no one knows except the Spirit of God" (1 Corinthians 2:11). What comfort! God knows us through and through and still loves us. Whom do you know on earth that could know every thought and action of your life and still love you perfectly? No tattletale can inform God of something that would alter His opinion of us. The Enemy himself cannot shed light before God concerning us. We are known, and we are loved. How silly then that we would even try to cover up. We can come clean before God and others. If the highest court in the universe has declared us loved and forgiven, even though we are fully known, certainly we can openly deal with failure and sin before others. God's knowledge of our griefs and difficulties is infinite. In knowing Him we get His infinite knowledge concerning our state, for it is in waiting on Him that we know Him.

What does His omniscience mean to the unbeliever? "Where can I go from Thy Spirit? Or where can I flee from Thy presence?" (Psalm 139:7). There is simply no place to hide. It is like God is saying to us, "You can pay Me now or you can pay Me later; however, you *will* pay." What a frightful thing to realize that God knows the very motives of the heart. "If I say, 'Surely the darkness will overwhelm [cover] me, and the light around me will be night,' even the darkness is not dark to Thee, and the night is as bright as the day" (Psalm 139:11–12).

THE GOD YOU CAN KNOW

HIS OMNIPRESENCE

Another perfection of God is His *omnipresence*. God is everywhere at once. "'Can a man hide himself in hiding places, so I do not see him?' declares the Lord. 'Do I not fill the heavens and the earth?' declares the Lord" (Jeremiah 23:24). What comfort! God is nearer to us than our own thoughts. People have said to me, "I just don't feel like my prayers are getting past the ceiling." First, we must understand that God is below the ceiling. Second, we should examine our hearts as to our loss of joy. Every child of God can take great comfort that God stays closer than a brother. He not only looks upon us, but He also gets intimately involved with us. The Christian cannot do anything without God's being there.

How we must grieve God! How we slander His name. Every sin committed is as though we did it right in front of the very throne of God. To unbelievers, this attribute is awful. He has seen all and knows all and someday will bring them into His full presence. All of their sins will be immediately exposed to Him who saw everything everywhere.

HIS GOODNESS

What about the *goodness* of God? Man, being limited to time, looks at immediate goodness whereas God looks at ultimate goodness. The goodness of God is seen through His daily provisions. How sad to see a Christian complaining when it is because of the goodness of God that he has anything. The ability to see God's goodness was an amazing characteristic of Paul's life. He believed he did not deserve anything; therefore, he appreciated everything and expressed himself with thanksgiving. He knew God in His goodness, and that made him say, "I have learned to be content in whatever circumstances I am" (Philippians 4:11). Find me a person content for no earthly reason, and you have found a delightful person to be with. He exudes the goodness of God.

For all eternity we will be discovering the great goodness of God. How could we receive such prizes as eternal life and daily provisions, and dare to complain? How could we ever disobey such a God? If a man gave you one million dollars, you would not spit in his face. You would immediately say, "Thank you," and ask, "What can I do for you!" How dare we receive such a gift as total forgiveness of sins and then not be indebted to the One who gave it!

What terror for the unbeliever to know—if he remains in that state on earth for all eternity and shuts himself off from God's goodness. One reason hell will be so bad is that it will never see a ray of God's great goodness. "For with Thee is the fountain of life; in Thy light we see light" (Psalm 36:9).

HIS HOLINESS

The *holiness* of God is another of His perfections. Because of His holiness, God can have no communion with sin. "Thine eyes are too pure to approve evil" (Habakkuk 1:13). His holiness means His majestic purity. Berkhof defines that holiness as "that perfection of God, in virtue of which He eternally wills and maintains His own moral excellence, abhors sin, and demands purity in His moral creatures."[7] The holiness of God is specifically revealed in His moral law. It stood out predominantly in the Law given to Israel. To be holy, God does not conform to any preconceived standard. He is the standard. Because He is holy, all His attributes are holy; that is, whatever we think of as belonging to God must be thought of as holy.

In Isaiah 6 when Isaiah saw the Lord, he shook greatly and was shattered to the very core of his being because he saw the holiness of God. God's perfection is seen in His holiness, and that perfection is the standard by which all mankind's behavior is judged (Romans 3:23).

God's own holiness has been put in His children (Ephesians 4:24). Those who have seen their sin and humbled themselves before His holiness have received the answer to sin's scars—that is, the blood of Christ—and are therefore holy. I am to be holy in my walk, but I am already holy in my position before God. The creature could do nothing to obtain the Creator's holiness. We take no pride in the gift but delight in such mercy. Sin is no longer an "abnormality." Sin is no longer a "problem of parental upbringing." Sin is anti-God! Willful sin tells God that we do not like Him, that we do not care about Him. Oh, the mercy and long-suffering of God, that He does not simply blot us out.

The sovereignty of God has to do with both His will and His power.

What would God's holiness mean to the unbeliever? It means that there is a standard. Things might be questionable to the person, but not to God. It is right or it is wrong! His holiness will be the plumb line by which all actions and thoughts will be judged. Sin is simply missing the mark of God's holiness (Romans 3:23). His holiness also means to the lost that the wrath of God will be known. God's holiness and wrath are inseparable. God's wrath is His utter intolerance of whatever degrades, demoralizes, or destroys. He hates iniquity as a mother would hate polio that would destroy her child. Those outside of Christ have the motto "Get it now and pay later." God's holiness tells us that the payment later is far greater than anything you could get now.

HIS SOVEREIGNTY

Another perfection of God is His *sovereignty*. There is a wealth of Scripture concerning this particular attribute of God. "For the Lord your God is the God of gods and the Lord of lords, the great, the mighty" (Deuteronomy 10:17). Other passages are 1 Chronicles 29:11–12; Nehemiah 9:6; Psalm 22:28; 50:10–12; Jeremiah 27:5; Acts 17:24–26; and Revelation 19:6.

The sovereignty of God has to do with both His will and His power. The sovereign will of God is the exercise of God's supremacy in the total course of human events. That means that God is absolutely free. No one and no one thing can hinder Him or compel Him or stop Him. He is able to do as He pleases always, everywhere, forever. To be thus free means also that He must possess universal authority. He is free from being caught off guard—free from changing His plans because of what the devil or man does.

Instead of seeing this attribute as doing away with our free will, we should rejoice. God is in total control. No move of nation against nation is done apart from His choosing. God looks at our past lives from a completely different perspective. God was accomplishing His will even through our own failures and sin. Are people free to choose for or against God? They are not free in the sense that they are unbiased toward God. Everyone is born with a bias against God. It certainly is not a fifty-fifty choice; that is, one does not grow up with as good a chance to choose for God as against Him. A person will choose against Him every time unless God moves first. Within His sovereignty there is clear indication of man's freedom throughout the Scriptures, but man's freedom has boundaries whereas God's sovereignty does not.

It is foolish to think that a man could turn aside the purposes of God. If you were standing on the top of a cliff with the water rushing in from the ocean, could you imagine yourself jumping down and pushing back the waves into the ocean? Of course not. Could you stand in a storm and as the bolt of lightning came through the sky, grab it and change its course? Of course not. Still more foolish is the thought that you could push back or change the determination of the Almighty.

Not only is God's will sovereign, but His power is, as well. That power may be called the creative energy of His nature. The sovereign power of God and God's other attributes work together. God's great power works within the realm of His holiness. My son once asked me why the Lord did not go ahead and save the devil—we would all be better off! That sounds good when you consider God's sovereign power, but does not fit with God's holiness. It might fit with God's mercy but not with His justice. God, being totally just, will have all things made right and fair when we see Him face to face. My failure, sin, and confusion do not change His chosen ends. What would it profit a man to spend any time trying to buck God's will? Could he win? Never!

The need today for the renewed study and knowledge of God is desperate. The cheap values of the world and even many of today's Christians are a clear indication that we know and love this world more than we do God. All the running after spiritual "highs" will fade during days of persecution. All that will remain is the stability and contentment that can only be obtained through knowing God. The very fact that we are more awestruck today with what God does than with who He is in Himself shows a weakness. God would have us say with John Wesley, "Thou, O Christ, are all I want; and more than all in Thee I find," and to exclaim with David Brainerd, "Farewell vain world, my soul bids you adieu; my Savior taught me to abandon you. Your charms may gratify the sensual mind, but they cannot please a soul for God designed."

Prayer: O God, Your amazing transcendent character makes me feel like a worm. But what a blessed worm to have a God like You. I am awed by Your majesty and glory when I get a glimpse of Your attributes. I know of nothing else to do but to humble myself before You. I give myself to You 100 percent. I take any glory that would go to me because of Your goodness and give it back to You. You alone are worthy. I would not choose to be exalted because of the work of Your hand. Show me Your great character in the days ahead—that I might know You, whom to know is life everlasting. Amen.

NOTES

1. Charles H. Spurgeon in Elon Foster, *Six Thousand Sermon Illustrations* (Grand Rapids: Baker, 1972), 294.

2. Louis Berkhof, *Systematic Theology* (Grand Rapids: Eerdmans, 1939), 41.

3. Ibid., 43–44.

4. Charles Hodge, *Systematic Theology* (London: James Clarke, 1960), 390.

5. Stephen Charnock, *The Existence and Attributes of God* (1853; reprint, Grand Rapids: Baker, 1979), 362.

6. A. W Tozer, *The Knowledge of the Holy* (San Francisco: Harper & Row, 1961), 61.

7. Berkhof, 74.

4

THE PERFECTIONS OF GOD (PART 2)

We ended the last chapter by discussing the perfections of God's sovereignty. That doctrine, which seems so terrifying to some, becomes the most precious when understood clearly. I suppose nothing illustrates it better than the book of Jonah. All of us are familiar with his ride in the fish. We have all heard it happened because he disobeyed God, and that was his punishment. That is true, but that is only a superficial understanding. Let us look briefly into that story where God's sovereignty is very evident.

From reading the account we already know that Jonah wanted out of God's will. In attempting to get "out," no one was hurt but Jonah. He was bent on not doing what God said to do, which was that Jonah should preach to Nineveh. Now we see that battle of Jonah's hard head against the sovereignty to God. Who would win?

Notice that everything in the story obeyed God except Jonah—the wind, the waves, even the heathen men who repented before Jonah. God even took the time to change those heathen men in order for Him to set Jonah straight. We see that Jonah tried to kill himself rather than do God's will. When he told the men to throw him overboard, that was what he was thinking would happen. He would drown, and it would all be over. God intervened all along the way to accomplish His purposes. I am sure when the fish swallowed Jonah, Jonah thought something like this, *Oh, no! All I wanted was to die.* You see, Jonah was contending with God's sovereignty. Jonah was learning a mighty lesson—*God can bless our obedience or judge our disobedience, but He will accomplish His will.* Jonah said, "I'm not going to the pagans." God said in return, "All right, but I'll accomplish My task anyway. You can disobey, but it will be according to My rules."

He is faithful, in control, and will keep His Word.

Jonah was a bit of an extreme case, but God's sovereign control can be clearly seen. Sovereignty does not imply that man can resist until the very end and then God will still press him, kicking and screaming, into the kingdom of heaven. God's sovereignty makes His grace irresistible, not in violating our wills, but in overcoming the resistance of our wills. He gently subdues and overcomes human resistance in order that we may gladly respond.

God's sovereignty means He is faithful, in control, and will keep His Word. We might not feel forgiven, but God's sovereignty demands that He keep His Word to forgive us. We can look at past failures and believe they were still under God's control. But that look convicts us of the time and money we wasted in our determination not to do His will. Jonah paid the fare to get away from God, whereas the "ship" heading for Nineveh was a free ride. Jonah never got his money back.

What conviction to the unbeliever! To think that he can have an argument before such sovereignty or to think that he can gain through rebellion is ludicrous. God's sovereignty says, "You can pay Me now or you can pay Me later, but you will pay Me!" How true in Jonah's case, and how true it remains today. "Hallelujah! For the Lord our God, the Almighty, reigns" (Revelation 19:6). "The Lord has established His throne in the heavens; and His sovereignty rules over all" (Psalm 103:19).

HIS FOREKNOWLEDGE

A perfection of God that goes with His sovereignty is His *foreknowledge*. He knows all things before they happen. There is nothing that catches God off guard. Everything about our bodies is known to God. The Bible tells us He even knows the number of hairs on our heads. Why did God bother to count the hairs on a person's head? He didn't! He intrinsically knows without counting. God does not keep a record. He knows all things. He never has to find it out first through a ledger.

Arthur Pink said this about foreknowledge: "The fact is that *foreknowledge* is never used in Scripture in connection with events or actions; instead, it always refers to persons. It is to persons God is said to 'foreknow,' not to the actions of those persons"[1] (Acts 2:23; Romans 8:29–30; and 1 Peter 1:2). That does not prove that God does not foreknow actions. It just makes individuals special in terms of God's meticulous foreknowledge.

No tragedy ever occurred that caught God sleeping.

Every move of God toward us reveals His careful plan of foreknowledge. The body is transparent before Him. "The darkness is not dark to Thee" (Psalm 139:12). Whispering will not muffle what is said. "Even before there is a word on my tongue, behold, O Lord, Thou dost know it all" (Psalm 139:4). There is no thought outside His awareness. "I know their works and their thoughts" (Isaiah 66:18).

What does His foreknowledge mean to the unbeliever? According to Hosea 13:12, sin is laid up against a future day of judgment. They are tampering with God's divine "layaway plan": Sin now and pay later! There is a future day when all of God's knowledge will be unmasked. The unbeliever hopes there will be some things God does not know about, but it will not be so. That person needs to read Romans 2:5–6 and then repent!

A lack of clear and scriptural views of this doctrine have caused among believers many erroneous ideas that have dishonored God. Because the doctrine runs across the grain of common sense it is questioned. Common sense is not the issue; it is God's character and glory.

HIS WISDOM

God is perfect in His *wisdom*. As the sun cannot be without light, neither can God be without wisdom. He has wisdom *originally*. Men acquire wisdom through experience; God has it by essence. He does not have to study or gain more experience. God has wisdom *perfectly*. He has absolutely no ignorance. He has wisdom *universally*. Men are wise in various things. God is wise in all things. He has wisdom *perpetually*. Man's wisdom fades near death. God's wisdom is perpetual. His wisdom is *incomprehensible*. The wisdom of one man may be comprehended by another. "Canst thou by searching find out God?" (Job 11:7, KJV). His wisdom is *infallible*. Even the wisest men fall short of their goals. God never fails.

God knows me! He knows every tear I cry. "Thou hast taken account of my wanderings; put my tears in Thy bottle" (Psalm 56:8). God knows every trial we go through, and His wisdom allows each to happen. Since God has an infinite amount of knowledge and wisdom, we should never say God made a mistake. Instead we should say that we do not know very much. If we knew that God did not know everything, what would we do that we do not do now? This doctrine has a way of "keeping us straight"!

What does God's wisdom mean to the unbeliever? There is the promise of accurate judgment (Romans 2:2). There is no way to hide from God (Jeremiah 16:17). It reveals the folly of human wisdom. The world thinks it is wise when it only knows what God has revealed. In other words, we know no more than He allows us to know.

HIS LOVING-KINDNESS

Another perfection of God is His *loving-kindness*. That is an attribute that every Christian receives proof of many times over. Comprehending the winsome attributes of God, such as this one, puts in balance the dealings of the Almighty with men. Concentrating on only His sterner perfections can make God something less than His complete revelation of Himself to us. The first time loving-kindness is mentioned in Scripture is in Exodus 34:6, when it refers to God as "the Lord, the Lord God, compassionate and gracious, slow to anger, and abounding in lovingkindness and truth." The evidences of loving-kindness are indeed plentiful. Our quick complaining when something small goes wrong should result in as quick praise for the multitudes of small provisions that we take for granted. "I have loved you with an everlasting love; therefore I have drawn you with loving-kindness" (Jeremiah 31:3). Isaiah 63:7 speaks of "the multitude of His lovingkindnesses." It is incredible that although we are so sinful we should be a part of such love. His lovingkindness is better than life itself (Psalm 63:3–5). Samuel Rutherford said it this way:

> What power and strength are in his love! I am persuaded it can climb a steep hill with hell upon its back; and swim through water, and not drown; and sing in the fire, and find no pain; and triumph in losses, prisons, sorrow, exile, disgrace and laugh and rejoice in death. When I have worn my tongue to the stump in praising God, I have done nothing to Him; for my withered arms will not go about his high, wide, long, and broad love.[2]

We may have overwhelming confidence in our God, who will never do anything to harm us. "How precious is thy loving-kindness, O God! And the children of men take refuge in the shadow of Thy wings" (Psalm 36:7). His loving-kindness motivates us to praise and prayer. "Because Thy lovingkindness is better than life, my lips will praise Thee" (Psalm 63:3). We can cling to this attribute of God when we have fallen in our spiritual journey. "Be gracious to me, O God, according to Thy lovingkindness" (Psalm 51:1). How could we spurn such love? How can we trust ourselves instead of God when we know His loving-kindness is toward us? Can we do anything else but be followers of God and walk in love ourselves (Ephesians 5:1–2)?

What does that loving-kindness mean to the unbeliever? He will never know the loving-kindness of God throughout all eternity. What he experiences here is all he will receive. Separation from God is separation from His loving-kindness.

The Perfections of God (Part 2)

HIS PATIENCE

Another perfect attribute is God's *patience*. That attribute is passed over by many without comment. Usually God's holiness, justice, and mercy get more attention. One reason for that could be that His perfection is far beyond our ability to comprehend it. We have clear limits in our understanding of patience. As someone has said, "How can a society that exists on frozen dinners, instant mashed potatoes, packaged cake mixes, and Instamatic cameras teach patience?" The answer is simple: Society cannot teach patience, but God can. Romans 15:5 says God grants us patience.

His patience is seen in His dealings throughout history. Remember how He waited during Noah's day for 120 years to pass before allowing the Flood. We marvel at His power revealed in that Flood. Why can we not see the 120 years of His name's being dishonored while Satan reigned, and wonder at His patience? Israel wandered for 40 years. We all know that if we were in God's position, their murmuring would have brought us to our limit within the first of the 40 years.

The prophets speak of God's fourfold dealings with His people. First, God always sent a preacher to ask *why.* "Why are you doing this against God?" Second, God always relayed through the prophets the *woe* of His heart. "How could you hurt God like this? Do you know that God weeps for such sin?" Third, God always sent the message of His continued patience. He would have the prophet tell the people that He was *waiting* for their repentance. Last, and only then, did God present to them His *wrath.* God's patience should astound every one of us. We should be amazed that we suffer so little for the consequences of our sin. Entire nations spurn His name and nothing happens. It is truly amazing that He does not strike them dead. How patiently He bears our own depraved conduct.

If a believer meditates on this perfection of God, he will find himself saying, "Thank You," many times over. "The Lord is slow to anger and great in power" (Nahum 1:3). God's patience and His power go hand in hand. To have patience one must have the power of self-restraint. God does not fly off the handle. If there is wrath, it does not come on quickly. The plagues on Pharaoh's people were illustrations of that powerful patience. Pharaoh would go back on his promise, but God would continue His prodding. God's wrath displayed at the Red Sea followed His patience throughout the long trial. Calvin himself said that this area of patience was his biggest problem. He called impatience the "beast" in his life. In contrast to all of us, "The Lord is gracious and merciful; slow to anger . . ." (Psalm 145:8).

The mercy of God can cause us to endure.

I can run to the patience of God when I have committed the same sin many times over. He is not looking for a reason to judge us; He is looking for a reason to bless us. Judgment requires the "cup of iniquity" to become full (Romans 1:18–26). Because I understand God's patience with me, I can comfort that friend who has never known true patience. I can lead him to the mildness of God. In light of such patience, how can we deliberately backslide? How can we be so insensitive to God? How can we sing in church as though we were bored with it all? How can we have such shallow gratitude?

What does God's patience mean to the unbeliever? It encourages him to find out why God's patience alone has not caused him to fall on his knees in repentance. Who else but a truly loving and patient God would have put up with his sin for so long? It should cause him to realize that God's patience will give way to an avalanche of wrath in the end. That attribute of God should also cause all of us to be more tolerant of one another. If God can put up with people, so can we.

HIS MERCY

Another perfection of God is His *mercy*. How many times have we heard the phrase "for His mercy endureth forever." The book of Psalms is a record of gratitude for this attribute of God. Joseph Addison in 1712 wrote:

> When all Thy mercies, O my God,
> My rising soul surveys
> Transported with the view, I'm lost
> In wonder, love, and praise.

Mercy, unlike grace, is shown to all of God's creation. Psalm 145:9 tells us, "His mercies are over all his works." There is also a special mercy of God on mankind. "In order that you may be sons of your Father who is in heaven; for He causes His sun to rise on the evil and the good, and sends rain on the righteous and the unrighteous" (Matthew 5:45). But, no one knows the mercy of God like the believer who has entered into God's covenant relationship. The unbeliever knows no mercy beyond the grave. God's mercy implies that there is already sin, for why should we need mercy if there were nothing to be merciful about? Thank God for His pity upon us. Our death in sin causes God to act on our behalf. First Peter 1:3 tells us, "His great mercy has caused us to be born again." His mercy never dries up. It endures forever.

Arthur Pink writes, "From the standpoint of the redeemed, the punishment of the wicked is an act of unspeakable mercy. How dreadful would it be if the present order of things should continue forever, when the children of God are obliged to live in the midst of the children of the devil. Heaven would at once cease to be heaven if the ears of the saints still heard the blasphemous, filthy language of the reprobate."[3] It is good news and great mercy that in the New Jerusalem "nothing unclean and no one who practices abomination and lying, shall ever come into it" (Revelation 21:27).

The mercy of God can cause us to endure. It will not quit; therefore, we cannot. We can endure others because God's mercy remains with us. There is an old story of a Jewish rabbi who consented to take a weary traveler into his house for a night's rest. After they ate, the rabbi asked the gentleman, "How old are you?"

"Almost a century old," the man replied.

"Are you a religious man?" asked the rabbi.

"No, I do not believe in God," said the gentleman.

The rabbi was infuriated. He opened the door and said, "I cannot keep an atheist in my house overnight."

The old man hobbled out to the cold darkness.

Later the Lord spoke to the rabbi. "Why did you let him go?" The rabbi replied, "I turned him out because he was an atheist, and I cannot endure him overnight."

God replied, "Son, I have endured him for almost one hundred years. Don't you think you could endure him for one night?"

The mercy of God endured us. Sometimes Christians become self-righteous; we imagine that we are living wonderful lives. We begin to believe that God blesses us because we are good. That is never true.

When the old Puritan saint Thomas Hooker was dying, his friends around his bedside said, "Brother Hooker, you are going to receive your reward shortly."

"No, no," he replied. "I go to receive mercy."

What does God's mercy mean to the unbeliever? Because of God's justice, good cannot result from evil. That contradicts the nature of God. Do you need the mercy of God? Could you live without it for all eternity? The unbeliever must one day admit that he is saved by God's mercy and not by his own self-effort.

HIS GRACE

Divine *grace* is another of God's perfect characteristics. That attribute is "extra special" to the believers because it is ours exclusively. God's grace is exercised toward the elect only. *Grace* defined according to Berkhof's *Systematic Theology* is "the unmerited goodness or love of God to those who have forfeited it, and are by nature under a sentence of condemnation."[4] To the degree that we are aware of the grace of God in our lives, to that degree we are walking humbly before God.

All through the Scriptures there is written the relationship of God's poured-out grace and man's response of humility. The reason is that grace is always unmerited. It demands a broken spirit to recognize it for what it is. Grace and works will never unite. "If it is by grace, it is no longer on the basis of works, otherwise grace is no longer grace" (Romans 11:6). One of my favorite phrases to express God's grace is in Romans 3:24. "Being justified freely by his grace" (KJV). The sinner is justified, that is, declared perfect before God. That is done without help from the sinner. It is by grace alone. We shall be singing of the grace of God throughout all eternity.

To save us by grace, God first had to have an eternal plan, and then He had to have the sovereign power to exercise that plan. I suppose from God's perspective, giving His grace to us must have given great pleasure. Think a moment. Here were creatures with absolutely no ability to get themselves out of the predicament they were in. They were dead in their sins, and they were not seeking God. Oh, the joy of exercising such powerful grace and taking the sinner from depravity to eternity in "the twinkling of an eye." Is that the reason the angels rejoice over the saving of one sinner? They rejoice in the saving grace of God, even though they know nothing of it. First Peter 1:12 implies that throughout all eternity we will be sharing with the angels the mystery of God's grace. They will be asking us, "What was it like to be made new?" The grace of God will get a lot of attention in heaven. A professing Christian who finds it necessary to apologize for his rebirth has missed the whole point of God's revelation on this attribute. Fanny Crosby wrote it this way:

> Someday the silver cord will break,
> And I no more as now shall sing,
> But O, the joy when I shall wake,
> Within the palace of the King.
> And I shall see Him face to face
> And tell the story—saved by grace.

Grace is a strong word for most people today. It demands a walk of humble devotion for those who know it. A person could not know the grace of God and be unconcerned if he walks with God or not. The very exercise of God's grace to my soul means that my soul is released from sin and put in bondage to His will. That is why Paul asks in Romans 6:1, "Are we to continue in sin that grace might increase?" Then he answers his own question. "May it never be!" (v. 2). It may very well take many believers the first 1,000 years of heaven to get over the shock of seeing who is not there.

Being a recipient of God's grace makes us as pure as He is. Sin is not just covered, but done away with. His grace is not cheap. It cost God His Son. We, therefore, have a large price tag on our heads, for we are rich in grace.

Nothing about grace gratifies the pride of man.

Under that conviction, can we continue in sin? Can we shrug off wrongdoing? Dare we treat God's grace as a license to sin more? Is it that cheap to us? Is it too much to ask that we give our few earthly years to Him who through grace has given us forever? Any other response than total commitment would be inappropriate. As J. I. Packer put it, "Those who think that because in Christ their sins are covered, they need not bother to keep God's law are desperately confused (see Romans 6). As it upsets a man more to learn that his wife is sleeping around than that the girl next door is doing it, so God is most deeply outraged when his own people are unfaithful."[5]

What does this grace mean to the unbeliever? He must be warned that grace is seen by the depraved mind as "foolishness" and as a "stumbling block" (see 1 Peter 2:7–8). Nothing about grace gratifies the pride of man. To trust self-effort to obtain divine favor is to undermine the entire meaning of grace. In hell there will be no grace. Hell will be sin's consequences poured out without a tinge of grace to cushion the blows.

HIS LOVE

As we near the end of investigating His attributes, we must not leave behind the *love* of God. God not only gives love, but He is love itself. His love is not just another characteristic, as we find among men, but it is His very nature. There is no condition put on that love. He does not love us "if" we love Him. He does not love us "because" we love Him. His love is spontaneous. "I have loved you with an everlasting love" (Jeremiah 31:3). God's love is not fickle. He does not turn off His love to teach us a lesson. It is eternal as He is eternal. His enduring love—even a child can comprehend it. Robert McCheyne wrote:

> Some of you are longing to be able to love God. Come into His love, then. Consent to be loved by Him, though worthless in yourself. It is better to be loved by Him than to love, and it is the only way to learn to love Him. When the light of the sun falls upon the moon, it finds the moon dark and unlovely; but the moon reflects the light, and casts it back again. So let the love of God shine into your breast, and you will cast it back again. The love of Christ constraineth us. "We love him, because he first loved us." The only cure for a cold heart is to look at the heart of Jesus.[6]

If one wants to measure the love of God, one must take a close look at Calvary. God's love has been shed abroad in our hearts. We are loved! There is nothing we can do to be unloved. It cannot happen. When the question comes, "How much does God love me?" the answer is found in Christ as He stretched out His arms on the cross and died for us.

How could we prefer the idols of this world—a person, a possession, or some pleasure? How could we run after its affection and spurn the love of God? How dare we question

God's love when we undergo trials? Eventually we will praise the Lord for showing us His side of the trial. Why can we not thank Him now by faith, knowing that we are loved and that nothing will be done apart from His great love for us? Are we loving others as an earthly picture of His divine love for us? Do we bring heaven to earth through loving others as we should? Seventy years is not enough time to express to God gratitude for His perfections given to us on earth. Since that is the case, why do we seek out other ways to spend our time rather than to give back to God what has been given to us?

What does His love mean to the unbeliever? First, the unbeliever never knows the real meaning of love until he finds it in God. All other loves on earth are cheap imitations of God's love. To love himself to the exclusion of loving God shows the sinner the hardness of his own heart. God's love can change selfishness into sweet sensitivity. We are loved! Christ's death proved it. How could we live without Him? The greater the love burns, the more sinful is its neglect.

HIS WRATH

One more notable perfection of God is His *wrath*. Christians apologize for that attribute. They believe that it does not fit with the rest of God's character. But God's hatred for sin is very real. His holiness would mean absolutely nothing if His hatred were less than what it is. Wrath is holiness stirred into activity.

Today we say very little to arouse or offend the callous and careless churchgoers among us. When John Wesley preached, he would hang the people's consciences over hell itself until someone would cry out in the service. Then he knew it was time to move on to God's grace. He had his hearers sweating for grace, and what relief when it arrived!

Today all of God's other characteristics are seen lightly because the wrath of God is not an issue. We find no sweating saints or sinners today. We are increasingly wrapped up with how the sermon affects "us" instead of "what does God think about this."

"Our God is a consuming fire" (Hebrews 12:29). True fear is needed in the hearts of God's children today—a fear that would keep us faithful to Him. Yes, His love overcomes wrath often, but no man in his right mind wants to pit the one against the other. "God is angry with the wicked every day" (Psalm 7:11, KJV). Paul said: "Knowing the fear [terror, KJV] of the Lord, we persuade men" (2 Corinthians 5:11).

How can God's wrath be comforting to the believer? It is comforting because daily he can count on being moved toward obedience to God through knowing His authority and wrath. We have a God who will not disregard sin, as might a mother who is tired of disciplining her children and disregards their misbehavior. He does not choose to turn His back on it. We have a God who so delights in purity that hatred for sin is its opposite. "If Thou, Lord, shouldst mark iniquities, O Lord, who could stand?" (Psalm 130:3).

What does His wrath mean to the unbeliever? The unbeliever should understand that the ungodly shall not stand in the judgment. If our Lord cried out under God's wrath on the cross, "My God, My God!" will not the unbeliever do the same? Who shall stand, when the Son of God Himself so trembled beneath the weight of God's wrath?

Francis Newport wrote these words as he lay on his deathbed:

Oh that I was to lie upon the fire that never is quenched a thousand years, to purchase the favor of God, and be reconciled to him again! But it is a fruitless wish. Millions of millions of years will bring me no nearer to the end of my torment than one poor hour. O eternity, eternity! Who can discover the abyss of eternity! Who can paraphrase upon these words, "for ever and ever"?[7]

Prayer: Father, so many seem to be ashamed of the gospel. Its revelation of Your grace, mercy, and justice seems to be a stumbling block to others. I want You to know, Father, that I glory in Your wonderful character. It has been made known unto me, and for that I am humbled and grateful. I would ask that You would make me a living example of one who knows You well. May Your Spirit move me deeper and deeper into that fellowship where I ask for nothing but yearn simply for You. Amen!

NOTES

1. Arthur W. Pink, *The Nature of God* (Chicago: Moody, 1975, 1999), 30.

2. Elon Foster, *Six Thousand Sermon Illustrations* (Grand Rapids: Baker, 1972), 432.

3. Pink, 88.

4. Louis Berkhof, *Systematic Theology* (Grand Rapids: Eerdmans, 1939).

5. J. I. Packer, *I Want to Be a Christian* (Wheaton, Ill.: Tyndale, 1977), 213.

6. Andrew A. Bonar, *Memoirs of McCheyne* (Chicago: Moody, 1947), 257.

7. John W. Lawrence, *Down to Earth* (Portland, Ore.: Multnomah, 1975), 54.

5

GOD'S HEART
EXPOSED
TO THE WORLD

The Bible is full of clear evidence that establishes the deity of Jesus Christ. God knew there would be a battle in the minds of men over accepting Christ's divinity.

God left us with numerous references concerning His deity. (1) The Bible applies to Jesus the Greek word *kurios* meaning "Lord," which was used in the Septuagint (the translation from Hebrew to Greek). That word in the Old Testament was the name for God Jehovah. (2) Phrases like "our Lord Jesus Christ Himself and God our Father" are used (2 Thessalonians 2:16). The verb is singular in that case as it is in 1 Thessalonians 3:11. Thus the prayer could be prayed to God the Father or Jesus. (3) The apostle Paul believed that Jesus would reappear as divine Judge at the end of the age, according to 2 Thessalonians 1:7–10. (4) In Mark 2 Jesus forgives sin. Only God has the authority to do that, as the scribes so noticeably were aware (Mark 2–7). (5) The gospel of John provides many proofs for the doctrine. "In the beginning was the Word [eternal one], and the Word was with God, and the

Word was God" (1:1). John 14:6 says salvation occurs only through Jesus Christ. Christ's preexistence and eternal oneness with God are clearly seen in the "I am" sayings throughout John's writings. "I am the light . . . I am the bread of life. I am the way." (See Exodus 3:14, "I am who I am.")

When Thomas was confronted by the resurrected Jesus, he confessed, "My Lord and my God!" (20:28). John also records Jesus' own sayings, "He who has seen Me has seen the Father" (14:9), and, "Before Abraham was born, I am" (8:58). The Jews tried to stone Him for those words. They knew He was claiming deity. (6) In Philippians the sentence "He existed in the form of God" was used to refer to Jesus (2:6). (7) Colossians 1:15 says Jesus "is the image of the invisible God." (8) Hebrews 1:3 says, "He [Jesus] is the radiance of His [God's] glory and the exact representation of His nature."

Robert Murray McCheyne put it this way: "There was an hour when God said, 'Let us make man.' But what an hour when God said, 'Let us save man.'" To make man was sheer joy. To save man was a painful confrontation between holiness and sin.

First Peter 1:18–21 places it all in perspective for us. "You were not redeemed with perishable things like silver or gold from your futile way of life inherited from your forefathers, but with precious blood, as of a lamb unblemished and spotless, the blood of Christ. For He was foreknown before the foundation of the world, but has appeared in these last times for the sake of you who through Him are believers in God, who raised Him from the dead and gave Him glory, so that your faith and hope are in God."

A study of the context of these verses will reveal God's holiness as the central theme. "I . . . am holy" (Leviticus 19:2). He immediately unites the theme of holiness with the ministry of redemption. By gazing into the mysterious depths of redemption, we shall behold the holiness of our Father. As a rule we do not look at the cross to find holiness. We find there mercy, forgiveness, love, and humility. Those things are certainly there, but at the core of the redemptive story is the holiness of the Father. When we celebrate Communion, or the Lord's Supper, we feel a sense of intimate love for the Savior, but have we ever felt the fierce, burning heat of holiness's touching sin?

Redemption is more than a tender Father's searching for His child; it is a holy God wrestling with the sin of the world. The conflict in redemption must be seen, or we do not understand it from God's perspective. Many of our popular songs reveal the fact that redemption obtained our forgiveness. That is good, but it hardly goes far enough. One does not find in those songs the bloody conflict, the taste of the bitter cup that our Savior drank. If we fail to comprehend God's holiness, we will not realize the immensity or the darkness of sin. Lower our sense of holiness, and our sense of sin is lowered. Take away sin's awful blackness and we rob the glory of redemption. The more one "lightens" sin, the more one uncrowns our Redeemer. If sin be a light thing, then our redemption was superficial.

A CHEAP REDEMPTION

Once sin is lightened and holiness hidden, we begin to cling to a cheap redemption. It is against that viewpoint that Peter raises such a mighty warning—"There was nothing cheap about it. You were not redeemed with corruptible things, but with precious blood, the blood of Christ." Did God become a man in order to show us how to love? Did He come to earth to reveal His tender heart toward us? Not primarily. He came at a great cost to Himself to launch a mighty war on sin in its immensity. If we are to see sin we must see holiness, shown to us in the "lamb without blemish and without spot."

In moving through the mystery of redemption, we should never become deaf to the Savior's words, "If it be possible, let this cup pass from Me," and, "My God, My God, why hast thou forsaken Me?" As long as we hear those cries from the Savior, we will not entertain a cheap redemption. We behold an unspeakable conflict where purity and depravity meet—where God who cannot look on sin became sin. Nothing but the cross could reveal the conflict. No other weapon could be used to fight sin. The Lamb of God hanging on the cross was the climax of the conflict. How much does God hate sin? Look at the cross and measure His hatred.

Christ is the central figure of biblical revelation. The cross is the central factor in biblical revelation. The Bible is a book about salvation from sin. Jesus is central because He is the One whom God uses to be His weapon in overcoming sin. All of God's perfections mean nothing to man if man cannot be saved from sin. To know and appreciate God, we must be able to receive Him fully. We cannot do that if sin is in the way.

No man can read Isaiah 53 without sensing something of that conflict between God and sin. In verses 4–6 the human side of the cross is represented. "Surely *our* griefs He himself bore, and *our* sorrows He carried. . . . He was pierced through for *our* transgressions, He was crushed for *our* iniquities; the chastening for *our* well-being fell upon Him, and by His scourging *we* are healed. . . . The Lord has caused the iniquity of us all to fall on Him" (italics added). Those phrases indicate that our Lord's death on the cross was an act of God, not just a deed of men. It was, therefore, an atonement, not just a crucifixion.

The next half of the same chapter reveals God's side of the conflict. Verses 8–12 say: "He was cut off out of the land of the living, for the transgression of my people to whom

the stroke was due. . . . The Lord was pleased to crush Him . . .
He would render Himself as a guilt offering. . . . By His
knowledge the Righteous One, My Servant, will justify the
many, as He will bear their iniquities. He . . . was numbered
with the transgressors; yet He Himself bore the sin of many,
and interceded for the transgressors."

Those aspects of the Atonement are seen from God's
point of view. Right in the center of those two groups are the
words "He is brought as a lamb to the slaughter, and as a
sheep before her shearers is dumb" (v. 7, KJV). The idea
throughout the passage is that the conflict was being borne
in the body of the Lamb of God. The battle was on. The Hebrew words for *bore* and *carried* both stress the idea of a
consciously endured pressure of weight.

Seeing the crucified Lord demands a crucified life.

In Gethsemane we see increased pressure in the conflict.
Sin and holiness are getting closer and closer. They will
meet at the expense of God. What amazing grace! Mark
14:33 tells us that Jesus "began to be very distressed and
troubled." The Greek phrase here means to be "astounded,
staggered, bewildered, or dumbfounded." Our Lord was
driven beyond Himself in anguish, struggling with the conflict of having sin laid upon Him for the first time in eternity.
J. H. Jowett says: "His fine, sensitive membrance of the soul
had in nowise been scorched by the fire of iniquity. No sin.
He was perfectly pure and healthy. No power had been
blasted by the lightning of passion. No nerve had been atro-
phied by the wasting blight of criminal neglect. The entire

surface of His life was as finely sensitive as the fair, healthy skin of a little child."[1] The more exact the purity of soul, the more exact the pain of sin. The suffering of that Lamb was not like the suffering any other sacrificial lamb had known.

"He is led as a lamb to the slaughter." Can any Christian heart ever get over that? Those nail-torn hands and feet are more marvelous than all the rest of His creation. The war the Lamb of God launches on our sin made us a slave to Himself. Seeing the crucified Lord demands a crucified life.

When one realizes what sin did to Christ, one has a better picture of the conflict between God's holiness and sin. At that time of Jesus' birth, He was sought out by Herod to be killed. The world was made by Him, yet the world would have nothing to do with Him. There was no room in the inn. There was no room in the hearts of men. They hated, rejected, and scorned Him. Because of sin, He was mistreated, persecuted, hounded, and taken to court.

We hate sin because of what it did to Jesus. He became sin for us (2 Corinthians 5:21). Can we truly envision the fairest Lord Jesus, the bright and morning star, the beauty of beauty, now a Lamb being led to slaughter? Do we not want to run to that crucifixion scene and rescue Him? But remember, we were the problem. We could offer nothing to help. It was all happening because of our sin. We could lend no hand to comfort or lessen the struggle. We only could add to the struggle. He, being the only One who was blameless, had to do it alone.

The types of symbols used to represent our Lord were ugly types. Isaiah 53:2 calls Him a "root out of parched ground." The Bible says, "As Moses lifted up the serpent in the wilderness, even so must the Son of man be lifted up" (John 3:14). He is likened to a hissing, crawling snake, as well as to an ox that is broken. Jesus, who knew all and had power to do all, had nowhere to run. He was broken. He was made the scapegoat. Mysteries were multiplied at Calvary: the veil was rent; the darkness came; the tombs opened up. All of creation reacted to that enormous conflict of holiness and sinfulness. Then Jesus cried out, "My God, My God, why . . . ?"

We hate sin because Jesus took the full cup while hell made its jubilee. The cross was stuck down in the face of hell itself. He who was fairest of all became a torn heap of flesh. In dying on the cross, He was laying down His life. No one was taking it. He controlled Himself until He gave up His last breath. He knew when it was "finished." The authority of those words tells us that He had won the conflict. Sin had lost. The seal of the Resurrection was needed to break sin's hold, but the battle was over, and sin would no longer block man from getting in on the perfections of God.

Back in Genesis 3 we have the record of God's cursing Adam and Eve for their sin. In that process God listed five objective consequences. (1) There would be thorns to hinder farming the land. (2) There would be sweat in work. (3) There would be pain. (4) There would be enmity between Satan and man. (5) Man would be separated from God. I am sure Adam listened carefully and was prepared to take the first four because of his sin; but when God told him that He would not walk with him anymore, I believe Adam would have begged God to remove that curse. He probably said, "God, I will take the pain and sweat, but don't separate Yourself from me. Please don't. You are all I want. We've been so close." Because of Adam's sin, God had to separate Himself from man.

THE CROSS

When we come to the cross, we see that the very things God cursed man with, Jesus, the Lamb of God, endured.

God laid on Himself the consequences of the curse to the very last degree. God said there would be "thorns." The Roman soldiers mocked Christ, placed a crown of thorns on His head, and then beat them into His skull. The curse involved sweat. In Gethsemane Christ sweat blood. The third curse was that of pain. No one has suffered more pain than the Lamb of God.

No one suffered more conflict with sin and Satan than Jesus.

Jesus suffered physically in six ways. One can beat men to death; lacerate them; wound them through penetration, as was done with the nails; kill them through perforation, as was done with the crown of thorns; kill through incision, as was done with the sword in His side; or kill a person through suffocation. That last way was what ultimately killed Jesus. The curse of pain put on Adam was totally fulfilled in Christ's death.

The curse of enmity between Satan and Adam was taken on as well by the "Last Adam," Jesus Christ. No one suffered more conflict with sin and Satan than Jesus.

Last, the curse of separation from God came to Jesus, also. On the cross those agonizing words rang out, "Why hast thou forsaken Me?" Every curse laid on man, Jesus bore in His own body.

Salvation is complete. That Lamb of God is God incarnate. He not only is to be exalted, but He is to be worshiped. Revelation 4 and 5 say that the same kind of praise and prayer that are offered to God are now offered to the

Lamb, the risen and exalted Lord Jesus, God the Son incarnate. In that pure worship up yonder, where the Lamb is "in the midst of the throne," He is worshiped not only as "Son of God," but as God the Son.

He alone is worthy to receive power, riches, wisdom, might, honor, glory, and blessing. The Lamb is central because He brought man into a position in which God could reveal Himself totally to him. Rejoice! We shall see Him even as He is.

The result of that great victory on our behalf by the Lamb of God is stated by Paul in Colossians 2. We have become those who have attained "all the wealth that comes from the full assurance of understanding, resulting in a true knowledge of God's mystery, that is, Christ Himself, in whom are hidden all the treasures of wisdom and knowledge" (vv. 2–3).

Prayer: Father, I am indeed grateful for the price paid for my salvation. The crucified Lord demands my crucified life. I give my life afresh to You. Like Paul, I accept the challenge to share Your sufferings. I desire to be so finely tuned to Your holiness that sin disturbs me and makes me determined to be all the more holy. Help me to be one of those who will stand in the gap even if it costs me my life. That would be a small price to pay for Your approval. Thank You for creating me new in Christ. Amen!

NOTE

1. J. H. Jowett, *The Epistles of St. Peter* (Grand Rapids: Kregel, 1970), 92.

6
WHAT MOTIVATES GOD?

"What Motivates God?" is a strange title. Since a major problem today in the business world, the educational system, and the church is lack of motivation, we can probably learn much from understanding how God is motivated. From one perspective God does not need any motivation. Being perfect within Himself, He needs nothing to get Him going. He is not at all dependent on outside or extrinsic motivation. In His relationships with His children, God has a definite intrinsic motivation. Some say that the love of God motivates all of His other attributes. Others say that the holiness of God is the motivation behind all His doings. What exactly does tie all of God's attributes together? What is it that makes God act as He does toward His children? It is my understanding from the Word of God that the answer to those questions has to do with His fatherhood.

Jesus expressed fatherhood as God's most important attribute. Let me explain why I believe that. I have already stated that it is impossible to have a healthy relationship with God without having a right concept of who He is. An incorrect concept of God will bring an incorrect response to Him. Likewise, a confused concept of Him will bring a confused response to Him. A distorted concept of God will bring a distorted response to Him. As Christians, you and I respond to the God that we know.

Peter Lord, pastor of Park Avenue Baptist Church, Titusville, Florida, said, "If a person believes that God gets all excited about nickels and noses on Sunday, then that person will respond by building a large church financially and in attendance. Many people think God is vitally interested in money. If the offering is bad, then God might not be able to do what He wants to do. Their concept of God is that God needs our money. Obviously, if God needs our money, then He is in bad shape!"

Whatever one thinks God is interested in will motivate one to get it done. Therefore, we must have a clear idea of what God's interests are.

THE NAMES OF GOD

God revealed His interests throughout the Old and New Testament. He revealed Himself not only through His glory and His attributes but also through the names of God. Those names describe the way God deals with us, as well as tell of the things that excite Him. "God is the incomprehensible One, infinitely exalted above all that is temporal; but in His names He descends to all that is finite and becomes like unto man."[1] The names of God are not names men have chosen about Him. They are names given to us by God about Himself. They give His personal revelation of His divine Being.

The first name we encounter in reading through the Old Testament is *Elohim*. It comes from the word *el* meaning

"lord, mighty, or powerful." "In the beginning *Elohim* . . ."
(Genesis 1:1). *Elohim* is the plural form of "mighty one." It
conveys the meaning "man gods." That Hebrew name de-
notes that God is so powerful that a million gods together
would still not produce His sovereign power. It is not trying
to prove Trinity, but rather immensity. Many people know
God as the powerful One. He can do anything. Since many
believe that to the point that they only perceive God sitting
on His throne in heaven, a mere object of power, there is a
need to see God through another one of His names.

Shaddai and *El Shaddai*. That name means "possessing all
power." *Elohim* stresses the greatness of God while repre-
senting Him as an object of fear and terror. *El Shaddai* stresses His blessing, comfort, and fruitfulness. *Elohim* tells us
God is powerful. *El Shaddai* tells us that His power is personal. "And may God Almighty *[El Shaddai]* bless you and
make you fruitful and multiply you, that you may become a
company of peoples" (Genesis 28:3). El Shaddai is used
forty-eight times in the Old Testament—mostly in the book
of Job. What a book for God to reveal His personal comforting power, a book filled with valleys, difficulties, and
defeats.

A further revelation of God was vouchsafed in His name
Jehovah-Jireh. That name means "God is our provider." "God
will provide for Himself the lamb" (Genesis 22:8). The
promise of God's provision for His children is now manifested.

Jehovah speaks of the self-existent, unchanging God. It
stresses His covenant-keeping faithfulness. "I am the Lord
[Jehovah], that is My name; I will not give My glory to another" (Isaiah 42:8). God has unchanging rules for us that
are for our own good. He desires the best possible life for
us, and that includes preventing us from doing certain
things. God can restore a person who has fallen, but blessed is
the person who has God as his preventer more than restorer.

In the name *Jehovah* we also see God's great love. "I [Jehovah] have loved you with an everlasting love" (Jeremiah 31:3). When we love someone deeply, it naturally causes sorrow to see our love rejected. "His [Jehovah's] soul was grieved for the misery of Israel" (Judges 10:16, KJV). That rejected love will, of course, reveal another aspect of the name *Jehovah,* that is, His holiness that judges and condemns our sin, and yet redeems us and makes us His heirs. The name *Jehovah-Rapha* means "our healer." "I will put none of the diseases on you which I have put on the Egyptians; for I, the Lord, am your healer" (Exodus 15:26).

In Exodus 17:15 we see another of God's names. *Jehovah-Nissi* means "the Lord is my banner." That is, the Lord is our victory. His name promises that to us. We can depend on that victory as surely as we can depend on His name.

Continuing through the Word of God, we come to *Jehovah-Shalom.* That name means the "God of peace" (Judges 6:23–24).

David in the Twenty-third Psalm gives us *Jehovah-Horhi,* meaning "Jehovah, my shepherd." The tenderness of the Shepherd-and-sheep relationship is still beyond explanation today. Books have been written on it, but the concept seems inexhaustible.

Jehovah-Shammah, meaning "God is there," is found in the last verse of the book of Ezekiel. God is present. What a note of victory to end a book full of such gloomy details!

God has used His names to unfold to us portions of His character. The problem is that we still do not have a complete picture. We still do not know how to tie them all together so that we understand God to be who He is.

Stephen Charnock in his volume *The Existence and Attributes of God* goes into great detail concerning the need for an adequate view of God. If we view God as powerful, then we might also view Him as being very impersonal. If our concept of God is that He is love, then we might think that we can do anything we would like and He will still love us. If our concept of God is that He will be our provider, then we might get heavily into debt, thinking that God will bail us out. If God is our healer, then we might abuse our bodies in order to watch Him heal. If a person views God as holy to the exclusion of the other attributes, then we will usually see him spending his life trying to walk a straight line while greatly fearing failure.

Our response to God is based on our concept of who He is. If God is primarily a teacher, then I must respond by being a good student. If God is primarily master, then I must respond by being a good servant.

Peter Lord writes:

> I was raised with the concept that Jesus is Lord. To me, God's function was primarily Lord, and that meant King or Captain. My concept of the church was that of an army, marching forth to war with Jesus Christ as the leader. Jesus is Lord and He wants a kingdom so the best thing we can do is to go out and conquer a kingdom. If God is primarily a Lord, then He is mostly interested in an army and the best thing I can do is be a good soldier. The best thing a good soldier can do is shoot down all the enemies he can shoot down. So I spent most of my time doing that and encouraging others to do so—to "go out and get 'em." I worked hard at taking territory for God. A king wants a kingdom. I was worn out from trying to win more ground for my Lord.[2]

How typical that is of so many dedicated Christians! Peter Lord goes on to say, "Have you ever noticed what happens to a Christian who has this concept of God when he can't find any enemies to fight? He begins to fight other Christians. An army officer does not demand that I love you; I just have to be a good soldier."[3]

Why does one aspect of God's character have to eliminate the others? It does not have to be that way. However, in order for that not to happen, we must have one concept of God that all the others fit into.

Jesus came to tell us that God is a Father.

When I talk with people, especially students, about their concept of God I am often amazed that to them one aspect of God excludes many other aspects. Churches are often guilty of the same thing. They emphasize one truth about God and soon are labeled accordingly. God has been put into their "responding box," that is, they respond one way in their relationship with God, and therefore God must be just the way they picture Him. If I view God as Lord primarily, then I must concentrate on being a good soldier. A soldier does not have to be concerned about loving the fellow next to him. If he is a good soldier, who cares about showing love or tenderness toward others, whether they be friend or foe?

GOD AS A FATHER

That leads us back to our original premise—what motivates God? What is God at the very center of His Being? I agree with Stephen Charnock, Peter Lord, and Lloyd Ogilvie when they suggest it is His fatherhood. "There is one attribute of God through which we are able to see all the other facets of Him. It serves as the viewpoint or table from which we are able to view all the other facets of His personality. God is first and foremost, above and beyond anything else, a *father*."[4] <u>Only with that view of God as central do the other concepts of God fit in perfectly.</u> All of the things we have studied about God thus far in this book are, in a limited sense, true of a good father. In an unlimited sense they are true of God.

Jesus came to tell us that God is a father, His favorite way of addressing God and speaking about Him. Sometimes it was "our Father"; at other times it was "your Father," or "My Father," or just "Father." It was the most prominent truth that Jesus taught us about God. The term is applied to God 189 times in the Gospels alone. Of those, 124 of them are found in John's gospel. When you think that Jesus while on earth had the option of revealing any of several key concepts of God to us, His revelation of God as Father becomes quite impressive. John 17 is one of the dearest passages of Scripture for the Christian. It speaks of the knowledge and unity we are to have with our Father.

Not only is God a good example of what a good father is, but Jesus is a good example of what a good son is. It is as though the counsels of heaven met prior to Christ's coming and decided to lay emphasis on that one aspect of God's relation to man.

A father wants a family. If we view God as a father, we will naturally respond by being good children, good members of the family. It is that response that puts all other responses in balance.

I am a father. I have four children spread into every age category from college age to kindergarten. As a father, I want my children to learn as quickly as they can. If they come home with a bad report card, I am disappointed, but not as disappointed as I would be if they did not love each other. If I were a teacher focusing on grades only, then my concern would be grades. Because I am a father I would

THE GOD YOU CAN KNOW

rather see C s for grades and have them love each other dearly than see A s with little or no love between them. If I were only a master of my household, then I would desire only their obedience to the letter. However, I am a father, and it is an even greater concern to me that they enjoy home and find it secure in every way. To see children happy and getting along with one another is a greater thrill to a father than seeing their performance on dos and don'ts.

As a family we are to love and care for one another. I can go to school with you and never love you. I can sit in a service with you and never really love you. Many are doing just that in their churches. I can go to war at your side and never love or care for you. But I cannot be in the same family with you and never love you. Only in the father-family concept does the church function as it should.

Believers have failed to see God first of all as a father. That is why the church is not functioning like a good family. James 1:27 tells us, "This is pure and undefiled religion in the sight of our God and Father, to visit orphans and widows in their distress." If God were not a *father*, He could never have said that. "If you're running an army, the last thing you want around you is a bunch of widows and orphans. All they will do is halt your progress. Orphans don't do very well as a rule in the classroom either. They require too much attention and care."[5] The weaker ones, if you are a teacher, are sent to a lower level. If you are the leader of an army, they are sent home. Teachers and leaders of that kind are interested only in performance. Is that not the church today in many places? It is performance oriented. That is fine if God has only one attribute, but He does not. Beware of the danger of intimidating others on the basis of performance.

What characterizes your life? Do you have a strong sense of family in your life and in your church? Is your church characterized by being an army or a classroom instead of a family? If you are a family, that does not mean that instruction and obedience are not required. Any effective father includes those in his upbringing of the children.

Another choice thing about a family is that the size never matters. A small family can be a family as well as a large one. God is not just concerned that we have more money and more people all the time. He desires that we *function* as a family, loving, caring, encouraging, and affirming one another into Christlikeness (John 13:35).

If the pastor views God primarily as a teacher, then the pulpit and the Sunday school become the most important things in the body. But, if the pastor keeps the father-perspective of God in focus, the church body will see Him as a teacher, healer, miracle worker, master, and more. A father can be all of those things, but the other aspects by themselves can not produce an effective father.

In 1 John, the author pictures as a father one who is mature. "I am writing to you, fathers, because you know Him who has been from the beginning" (1 John 2:13). Our image of a father is very special. We can think of God and still be left cold somehow. We cannot think of a "father" in the same way. Jesus came to tell us that there is nothing on the heart of God more than that we know Him as our Father.

On the basis of the counseling I do, I would say that the two greatest problems among Christians are a lack of understanding their position in Christ and a lack of knowing God as their Father. They have no family image; therefore, they feel cut off from other family members—members of the body of Christ, as well as feeling alienated from God. Our fellowship is made solid only as we renew our thinking about God. What grief it must bring to God's heart for us to cast an image on Him that is not true.

A man can be a teacher without being a father, but a true

father will be a teacher. A man can be a lord without being a father, but a true father will be a good director of the home. A man can be a good provider without being a good father, but a true father will be a provider. It all fits. That is what motivates God—the delight in being a great Father to His children on earth! What a joy to God's heart when we respond as Jesus did when He was in Gethsemane. It was as if He said, "I know it's going to hurt, but You are my Father, and I know You will be everything that I need. I will trust You."

God made us to enjoy Him.

In my own family the greatest times with my children have been crazy times that only a family could enjoy. Times when we just go outdoors and tumble through the leaves with each other. Times when my son Johnny and I have played the whole evening away with some small creative object. Times when my sons and I just grab each other and hang on each other's neck. Teachers and pupils do not do that; neither do sergeants and privates. There have been times when my little Ann, who is now nine, and I have gone on dates together. We come home with hearts so full of love for each other and so full of laughter that the joy of the Lord is our strength for days afterward. There have been times when we as a family sing at the top of our lungs. Only fathers take time for such activities.

God made us to enjoy Him. It is difficult to always enjoy a teacher, or a lord, or a commander of an army. God is our Father, and we are to enjoy Him forever. The family concept in heaven will be perfect in every way. Heaven on earth is the ability to bring that concept to our own hearts, friends, and churches. (Is your church characterized by a sense of family, or is it an army or a classroom?) What a comfort to enjoy God like that! I can act as a child and treat Him as a father. I am free to fail, free to speak what is a concern to me, free to be myself, free from fear, free from guilt.

"See how great a love the Father has bestowed upon us, that we should be called children of God; and such we are. For this reason the world does not know us, because it did not know Him" (1 John 3:1). What is that verse implying? Precisely that we are not understood by the world, because we are to have such a strong family as well as a strong father image in our lives. The world is alienated, isolated, and on its own egocentric expedition. There is no unifying completeness to people's lives. They have not been placed in a family.

The results of thinking in any terms other than that of God as our Father are rebellion or fear of failure. If you have no family concept of love and protection of one another, you will walk a tightrope spiritually before God and before others.

I have learned that above all else I am to be a father to my children. (I am having a great time doing it.) I can go off with my children for days at a time and not feel like I am neglecting the ministry. I, like God, am to be primarily a father, not a minister.

I would challenge you to do something if this chapter is still a bit "foggy" to you. Read the gospel of John carefully during the next month and ask God to show you His fatherhood. When that is fully understood, I am sure you will never really recover from it.

Prayer: Dear Father, I again say, "Thank You," for revealing Yourself to me. I long to know You in Your fullness. Thank You for accepting me as Your child. Make me very sensitive to Your desires for me. Allow me to see You as the great God You are, but always through the image of Your being my Father. Thank You for the times of just loving each other as we do. Let me enjoy You as You desire that I do. Make this very day a delight to Yourself as we share and care together. In Jesus' name. Amen.

NOTES

1. Louis Berkhof, *Systematic Theology* (Grand Rapids: Eerdmans, 1939), 47.

2. Peter M. Lord, "Bible Study—God: The Father," *Fullness Magazine,* July-August 1979, 19.

3. Ibid.

4. Ibid., 20.

5. Ibid., 21.

7

GOD:
I WANT
TO WORSHIP YOU

The first thing God did after the fall of man was to seek out the lost one. He called to Adam, "Where art thou? Adam! Adam! Where art thou?" That was not the call of a policeman but of a tenderhearted father. In a way, God was experiencing a sense of loss. God created us to know Him. Now, Adam was cut off from communion with God and wanted to hide from Him. Adam had always enjoyed God, but at that point he could not bear to see Him. God's voice continued to echo through the Garden. It was a voice of grace, mercy, and love. Adam should have been seeking God, for Adam was the transgressor. After falling Adam should have gone all through Eden crying, "My God! My God! Where art Thou?"

WHAT IS WORSHIP?

God created man to worship Him; however, through his own sin man chooses to worship everything else but God. He hides from God and tries to eliminate God from his thinking. Christians often sing worshipful hymns in a "worship" service, and we call that worshiping the Lord. What is worship? And how does one worship the Lord? This chapter should assemble for us a skeleton outline on worshiping God, and the following chapters will provide the "meat" for the skeleton.

We often hear sermons about working for Jesus, but there is a paucity of sermons on worshiping Him.

It is possible to know a great deal about the Bible and not know the God of the Bible. You can even know a great deal about godliness without knowing God. Both Jeremiah 9:23–24 and Hosea 6:6 tell us that there is nothing more important than the knowledge of God. I hope you caught the word *nothing* in that last sentence. There is no book greater than the one that causes you to know God better. There is no material blessing that can bring contentment and enjoyment like the knowledge of God.

People sometimes ask me if I have met a famous person. They will say, "Have you met 'so and so'?"

"No," I reply, "but I know God!"

How exciting to know God! The references to worship throughout the Word of God are extensive, as evidenced by the fact that the longest book in the Bible—Psalms—is dedicated to that theme. God wants us to know Him in order that we can worship Him. You might ask, "Why should we worship God?" God knows that it is in the act of worship that He draws near to us, communicating His person to us, and sharing His secrets with us.

My son Steve came into my office one day. Usually, when I am in the office with the door closed, it means that others are to remain outside the door. This time Steve just barged in. He sat down quietly, and I asked him what he wanted.

He told me that he did not want anything. He said, "I just want to be with you."

"You just want to be with me!" I said. "You don't want five dollars?"

"No."

"You don't want to see if you can go out tonight?"

"No."

"You don't want help in your homework?"

"No, I just came to be with you."

Communion with God is the one need of the soul beyond all other needs.

How often do we do that with God? So many of us barge into His presence and share with Him our shopping list of prayer requests and then get up and leave. We fail to sit and just enjoy Him. We fail to become fascinated with Him, to adore Him and admire Him. We would never do such a thing in a doctor's office. We would not run in, tell him our problems, and run out. We would sit and wait for his diagnosis. Whereas the doctor is always busy God is never too rushed just to sit and talk. Oh, that God would free the Christian world from treating Him like a spiritual Santa Claus. He longs to give Himself much more than any gift. George MacDonald writes beautifully about why prayer is so necessary:

> "But if God is so good as you represent Him, and if He knows all that we need, and better far than we do ourselves, why should it be necessary to ask Him for anything?" I answer, What if He knows Prayer to be the thing we need first and most? What if the main object in God's idea of prayer be the supplying of our great, our endless need—the need of Himself.

. . . Hunger may drive the runaway child home, and he may or may not be fed at once, but he needs his mother more than his dinner. Communion with God is the one need of the soul beyond all other needs: prayer is the beginning of that communion, and some need is the motive of that prayer. . . . So begins a communion, a talking with God, a coming-to-one with Him, which is the sole end of prayer, yea, of existence itself in its infinite phases. We must ask that we may receive: but that we should receive what we ask in respect of our lower needs, is not God's end in making us pray, for He could give us everything without that: to bring His child to his knee, God withholds that man may ask.[1]

Blessed is the one who desires God rather than what He gives.

All through the Bible, when God wanted to bless a people, He did it by finding worshipers. Men would worship the Lord and get to know God's secrets for their people. There is a need for such men. We are fast approaching the day when we will be beyond preaching. Already, dynamic truth rolls off people like water off a duck's back, despite the fact that they are listening to tapes, going to seminars, attending conferences, and reading books more than any previous generation. What we need to realize is that truth never becomes ours until it becomes us. We can hear someone else's truth all day long, but until it becomes ours, it is still their truth.

You can search the Scriptures in vain to find God seeking anything other than worshipers. God gives men the gifts to do many things, but when it comes down to the Father's seeking out individuals, He always seeks those who worship Him. "But an hour is coming, and now is, when the true worshipers shall worship the Father in spirit and truth; for such people the *Father seeks to be His worshipers*" (John 4:23, italics added).

Moses went up on the mount for forty days and nights to meet with God. In that time he had a revelation of who God was, who Moses was, and what to do with God's people.

Stephen, in defense of the gospel before the Sanhedrin, spoke of the God of glory's appearing to Abraham, in Acts 7. He told the Sanhedrin that Abraham's encounter with God had caused him to leave his country, his comforts, and his comrades with no questions asked.

In Genesis 22:5 Abraham displays his own understanding of worship. It was the time for Abraham out of obedience to God to offer his very own son to die. Abraham left his servants behind and told them that he and his son were going up the mount to worship the Lord. Imagine calling the sacrifice of your own son a worship experience. God never intended to have Isaac killed by his father. God was testing what He loves to test in every child of God, that is, our willingness to sacrifice. All worship involves sacrifice, whether it be our time, our own egos, or possibly even our goals. It is God's desire for us to let go in order for us to receive from Him; however, His person is worth any sacrifice we would encounter.

MOSES AND WORSHIP

Exodus 33 is probably the Bible's greatest chapter on worship. It gives Moses' personal struggle with learning the lesson of worship. Moses makes a request before the Lord: "Now therefore, I pray Thee, if I have found favor in Thy sight, let me know Thy ways, that I may know Thee" (v. 13).

God answered Moses: "My presence shall go with you, and I will give you rest" (v. 14).

Moses seemed to get a bit frustrated with God. He told the Lord that he expected God's presence, but desired more, that is—God *Himself.*

After that explanation from Moses, the Lord said, "I will also do this thing of which you have spoken; for you have found favor in My sight" (v. 17).

Then Moses was free to pray, *"I pray Thee, show me Thy glory!"* (v. 18, italics added).

Did Moses receive God's glory? Yes. Hebrews 11:27 tells us, "He endured, as seeing Him who is unseen." What is the key to endurance in the Christian life? It is worship. The book of Hebrews makes that theme absolutely clear. It is a book written to condemn the worship of anything, even good things, outside of God's character.

Today the saints cannot endure much. We constantly talk about "our hurts," "our feelings," "our self-pity," and "our rejection." If we were to get a glimpse of God's glory, we would quit that kind of nonsense. Moses was not satisfied with having God's presence go with him. Though it would have been enough for most men, it was not for Moses. He wanted to know God's full glory. It was that great drive in his life that impressed God to share His glory with Moses. Has God ever shared His glory with you? You will never know what that means outside of true worship.

Exodus 33 is just one chapter in a great book on worship. After the first eleven chapters, the results of redemption are enumerated throughout the remainder of the book. Some of those results are guidance, joy, victory, and the supplying of our needs. But more emphasis seems to be placed upon worship than upon the manifestations of His power in us. Obedience, for example, was given great emphasis throughout the Ten Commandments, but worship in comparison received a greater overall emphasis. God used Exodus 25 to 40 to get the people ready for the greatest result of redemption—the worship of the Redeemer.

Another passage that gives extra insight into God's desire to be near us is found in Luke 10. The story of Mary and Martha is really quite humorous. "Now as they were traveling along, He entered a certain village; and a woman named Martha welcomed Him into her home. And she had a sister called Mary, who moreover was listening to the Lord's word, seated at His feet" (vv. 38–39). Notice the position of Mary in relation to the Lord. She was in a position of worship.

"But Martha was distracted with all her preparations; and she came up to Him, and said, 'Lord, do You not care that my sister has left me to do all the serving alone? Then tell her to help me'" (v. 40).

Imagine any person's having the audacity to command Jesus to do something. Why did Martha act that way? She was playing the role of any one of us who gets distracted doing things for God and loses the priority of worship.

Notice the Lord's response to Martha. "Martha, Martha." I am convinced that it would have been bad enough for the Lord to have said, "Martha." When He added another "Martha," you know she expected trouble. Jesus went on to say, "You are worried and bothered about so many things; but only a few things are necessary, really only one, for Mary has chosen the good part, which shall not be taken away from her" (vv. 41–42).

The worship of God involves three basic activities.

Notice our Lord's "countdown." He goes from "many things" to a "few things" to "one thing." The Christian life is full of many duties—a few are important. *However, only one* is *absolutely mandatory*—the worship of God. Jesus Himself said that this "shall not be taken away" from us (Luke 10:42). Everything else we worship will fade away.

The apostle Paul gave us the great essential in his statement of the goal in his life: "That I may know Him" (Philippians 3:10). He talks in that chapter about putting no confidence in the flesh, about experiencing loss and handling it, and about knowing God's will for one's life. Those three areas are the largest stumbling blocks among Christians today. Paul conquered them all through the worship of God. It is in knowing Him that we find true humility, not just pious pride. It is in knowing Him that we really rejoice and not just put on a smile. It was in knowing Him that Paul found God's ways. The secret of guidance is the guide. Get to know Him, and you will not miss His ways.

There are a few passages in the book of Revelation that must be examined before we can say we have covered the subject of worship. In chapters 4 and 5 we get a glorious glimpse of God's person being worshiped.

> And the four living creatures, each one of them having six wings, are full of eyes around and within; and day and night they do not cease to say, "Holy, holy, holy is the Lord God, the Almighty, who was and who is and who is to come." And when the living creatures give glory and honor and thanks to Him who sits on the throne, to Him who lives forever and ever, the twenty-four elders will *fall down* before Him who sits on the throne, and will *worship Him* who lives forever and ever, and will *cast their crowns before the throne,* saying, "Worthy art Thou, our Lord and our God, to receive glory and honor and power." (Revelation 4:8–11, italics added)

That passage clearly sets forth what it means to worship the Lord. The worship of God involves three basic activities. The first basic activity of a worshiper of Jesus Christ is to *fall down.* Every time you see worship being exercised, you see a falling down. "Come, let us *worship and bow down*" (Psalm 95:6, italics added). Even the devil knew that was mandatory for worship. "The devil took Him to a very high mountain . . . and he said to Him, 'All these things will I give You, if You *fall down and worship me*'" (Matthew 4:8–9, italics added). There is no worship without humbling ourselves.

I often hear people pray, "Lord, humble me!" I think it is a very poor prayer. First of all, you would never really want God to do it, and second, it is not scriptural. The Bible makes clear that we are to humble ourselves. Five times the New Testament tells us to humble ourselves and He will exalt us. God is not in the humbling business; however, God will humble us if we do not humble ourselves first. Blessed is the man who humbles himself.

A man cannot worship God and be controlled by his own pride. For that reason the Bible has quite a bit to say on the sin of pride, affecting our ugly, self-centered ego—that part of us that refuses to have another person exalted, except where it would benefit us. In the list of sins in the book of Proverbs, pride has preeminence. How could any Christian be filled with pride when the beginning and end of his Christian life had nothing to do with him? "What do you have that you did not receive?" (1 Corinthians 4:7). Look at the cross, and you will see it is all of God. Look at heaven, and you will see it is all of God. Anything that begins with the cross and ends with glory has to kick pride right out of us. "But if you did receive it, why do you boast as if you had not received it?" (1 Corinthians 4:7). The very character of Satan is pride. The middle letter of the word *pride* is I. The middle letter of the word *sin* is I. The devil is "self-made." Woe to the person who thinks he is!

The word *humility* has two meanings, one negative and the other positive. The negative meaning is that I must give up my right to myself. Whatever right I have—the right to marry, the right to remain in America, the right to buy what I want—must be given up. It is the right that must be given up. That means the attitude behind having things must be laid down. Can I do without and never question God or get detoured from His will? Have I laid down my rights to the point that I wholly and honestly worship Him alone? That is the first meaning of the word *humility*.

The positive meaning is that I must have a willingness to be ruled. Often, it is our pride that rejects others' telling us what to do. The thought that another would expose faults or suggest a better way to do something can be traumatic to the proud person. He sees no need for correction, no need for others to watch over him, no need for being ruled. That attitude carries into every walk of life, even the church. As a result, division takes place, and the character of God is belittled.

It should be no surprise that Paul's greatest chapter on humility is Philippians 2 and his greatest chapter on worship is Philippians 3. The one leads to the other. There must be a falling down before there can be true worship.

Recently I was at the University of Georgia speaking to several hundred students. I brought up a touchy subject—I asked them if they prayed on their knees often. Obviously, I was speaking to Christians. The picture they gave me was this: A roommate would be walking down the hall, and the Christian would be on his knees in the room. When the roommate touched the door handle, the Christian would bounce up and look out the window like nothing was happening.

Why not stay kneeling? It goes against the grain of every prideful bone in us. I am not insisting that it is mandatory to pray on one's knees to demonstrate humility, but it helps. When my boys and I pray together, we always get on our knees and usually grab each other during or after the prayer. We humble ourselves before God and each other and then commit our love to one another before we go.

Many times when we think of giving up our own rights or being willing to be ruled, we start accusing the other person. We say, "My husband should hear this, because his god is overwork." Or, "My wife should hear this, because her god is money." Or, "So and so has not given up his rights in this or that area."

The obvious things are not necessarily the most dangerous. Pride has many forms; the less obvious forms are the most dangerous. Immediately we think of the gods of money, overwork, and material possessions. What about the god of "false expectation"—expecting what someone is not giving and therefore assuming one has the right to complain or get angry? What about the god of having our eyes on other people? They fail us; therefore, we fail also. What about the sin of putting our eyes on circumstances? Things go wrong; therefore, we hold the right to be disappointed instead of being content in all things. No worshiper of Jesus Christ desires to cling to his own rights.

The second basic activity of a worshiper of Jesus Christ is to "*cast [your] crowns before the throne*" (Revelation 4:10, italics added). I wish I could see you right now as I ask the next question. How many of you have crowns? I suppose most of you would deny having many or any at all. But a "crown" is anything that exalts the wearer. If it draws attention to the person wearing it, then it is a crown.

I have been blessed with several crowns. My wife is a crown. I often hear great compliments paid her. People will say, "Your wife is so in love with the Lord, so discerning, such a good counselor, such a good cook, and is so full of life." You cannot give my wife a compliment without giving me one. (Notice, she married me, not you!) My wife, therefore, becomes a crown in my life. She exalts me by being such a choice wife and mother.

A teacher once told me that she wished she had a room full of students like my Johnny. I wanted to tell her that Johnny got it all from me! When my children have a reputation for good, it exalts "ole dad." Now, I realize that many times my children are thorns, but many times they are my crowns.

My job could be a crown. If I do it well and get complimented for it, it becomes something that exalts me. If I can play an instrument well, then people exalt me for that. It is not wrong to accept a compliment. Sometimes people will deny a compliment when I give it to them. They will say, "Oh, no, I can't really play very well." (I always want to tell them that I do not appreciate being called a liar. That usually wakes them up!) We are not to deny that we have talents, gifts, and crowns, but we are to "cast them before the throne."

These are dramatic words: "Cast them before the throne." In other words, be sure that every crown you have is laid before the Lord. He may touch it, take it away, or re-do it, but you will not complain or get detoured from His will, because He chose to alter your crown. Could you say that is true of all your crowns? My wife must be laid before the throne. If God were to allow her to die, would I question God's will because of it? Not if I have "cast [her] before the throne." She is not mine, and I have no right to claim her over God's will. My children are a crown. Are they before the throne to the extent that they could be taken from me and I would never question God? Could God touch your job or mine and possibly take it away? Would you question God because of it? If you would, you are still not a worshiper of Jesus Christ. No man who worships Jesus Christ ever wants to be exalted. The more I am taken up with Him, the less I am going to demand that my crowns stay untouched.

We can tell that the apostle Paul was a worshiper of Jesus Christ. Second Corinthians 12 tells us that he had an experience of going to heaven and coming back. He didn't tell anyone for fourteen years. What a crown to go up to heaven and come back. Imagine trying not to tell people. Paul seems to have had little difficulty in holding back from self-exaltation. He was a worshiper of Jesus Christ and was content not to speak of himself or his revelation.

You will notice that these phrases are dramatic—"Fall down" and "Cast [your] crowns." God did not say that worshipers necessarily "kneel down." They *fall down*. God did not say that worshipers "lay down" their crowns. They *cast them down*. There are no reservations in those actions. We are face to face with God!

There is a third and last basic activity of a worshiper of Jesus Christ. They *worship Him*. They tell the Lord His "worth-ship." To worship means to tell God His worth. "Doesn't He already know?" we might ask. Yes, He knows, but it is in the act of worship that He reveals Himself to us. It is also in the act of worship that we become what we worship. We can talk about becoming like Jesus Christ all our lives, but until we worship Him aright, we will stay basically the same. The twenty-four elders cried out, "Worthy art Thou, our Lord and our God, to receive glory and honor and power" (Revelation 4:11). When men seek glory, honor, and power, it causes war, divisions, divorce, and disharmony. No worshiper of Jesus Christ ever desires to rob God of His glory.

Get alone often just to sit and tell the Lord what He is worth to you. My wife does that through writing letters to the Lord. I enjoy worshiping through hymns in a hymnbook or through the Psalms. Others I know have what is called a "Praise Page" in their devotional notebooks. It is a page on which God's worth and many of His attributes are listed. The point is clear. Worship is mandatory. It is the only essential activity on earth. It will not decrease other things that are of God but will add more meaning to them. We must humble ourselves, cast our crowns before the throne, and tell the King of kings His worth.

Prayer: Lord, I cannot worship You without feeling a sense of inadequacy in doing so. How can I worship and give adequate praise to such a God? I am understanding that it is that inadequacy that thrills You the most. In my weakness, You desire to make me strong. I will trust You, O God, to make me a worshiper of You. Teach me to get alone often just to enjoy who You are to me and who I am in You. Thank You for creating me for that purpose. I give myself to You for the completing of this high calling for my life. Work it in me, I pray. In Jesus' name. Amen.

NOTE

1. C. S. Lewis, *George MacDonald: An Anthology* (New York: Macmillan, 1978), 41.

8
GOD'S TESTIMONY OF US

We move now from what we are to think about God to what God thinks about us. It is a wonderful thing to hear a person give testimony of what the Lord means to him. How much more wonderful is it to hear testimony of what we mean to the Lord from the Lord Himself! Many Christians are still stumbling over the truth of our position in Christ. The knowledge and appropriation of that one truth alone should pick any Christian off the earth and transcend him to the heavenlies. What does God think of us? Let us allow Him to give His testimony.

CONVICTION, NOT CONDEMNATION

God's testimony concerning us unfolds as we look into our position in Christ. Why is there such a need to know our position? First of all, how could any book be written on God as Father and not include the position of His children? The knowledge of that truth will produce freedom from spiritual intimidation in the Christian life. A major problem today is that either we are intimidated by another's super-spirituality or we intimidate others by our own spirituality. There is a right way to feel convicted, but it is never right to feel like a second-class Christian. Knowing our position in Christ will free us from guilt, as well as reveal to us the difference between condemnation and conviction. The latter is of God, and the former never is.

Understanding our position with Him frees us to be ourselves. So many people are living other people's Christianity. They are concentrating so hard on being like someone else that they fail to be themselves. Their own personalities get swallowed up, and they walk a tightrope, living a boxed-in Christian life. The truth of our position in Christ will free us from insecurity, from the lack of confidence, and from fear. The fear of missing God's will will fade away. The fear of the past will go. The fear of the future will have to flee, all because of that one glorious truth, which God meant for us to grasp firmly.

Most still think of Christianity in terms of what it forbids. When they consider Christianity, they think of what they are to be separated from instead of thinking with Paul what they are separated unto. If we are merely separated from, then Christianity takes on more repression than expression. It adds weights instead of supplying wings. Zinzendorf said, "No one is holier than a sinner who has received grace."

The New Testament uses five terms to summarize our salvation: (1) justification, (2) redemption, (3) reconciliation, (4) forgiveness, and (5) sonship. In seminary those five terms are given several months of study under the heading of "soteriology," which simply means the doctrine of salvation.

What a doctrine soteriology is! Let us look at those five terms and how they apply to us. In *justification* we stand before God as sinners declared righteous after being accused.

In *redemption* the sinner stands before God as a slave and is granted freedom by ransom. In *reconciliation* the sinner stands before God as an enemy who becomes a friend. In *forgiveness* the sinner stands before God as a debtor whose debt has been paid in full. In *sonship* the sinner stands before God as a stranger who is made son. Doctrinally, that is our position before God Himself.

We must understand the difference between repentance and remorse.

When we were saved, everything was taken care of. Notice how redemption deals with the root—our nature, and forgiveness deals with the fruit—our sins. Notice how reconciliation deals with condition—we were enemies, and sonship deals with our position—no longer strangers. God took care of everything: root, fruit, condition, and position. No one is holier than a sinner who has received grace.

Before we can go into the heart of the meaning of our position in Christ, we must understand the difference between repentance and remorse. The former is a word showing true conviction. The latter is a word involving only condemnation. The devil will condemn us, even our friends will condemn us, but God never does; He only convicts. Remorse, or a feeling of condemnation, carries with it no remedial or redeeming qualities. A remorseful person is very sorry for his wrongs, but he has never taken those wrongs to the cross to be set free from them. His past and present sins still haunt him.

The Scriptures make a clear difference between remorse

and true repentance. "I now rejoice, not that you were made sorrowful, but that you were made sorrowful to the point of repentance. . . . For the sorrow that is according to the will of God produces a repentance without regret, leading to salvation; but the sorrow of the world produces death" (2 Corinthians 7:9–10).

Paul was saying that it is a terrible thing to see a person regret his past, because he is still in bondage to it. The world's sorrow produces that kind of condemnation and fear. Paul said he rejoiced that those people knew true repentance. They had been freed. "For behold what earnestness this very thing, this godly sorrow, has produced in you: what vindication of yourselves, what indignation, what fear, what longing, what zeal, what avenging of wrong! In everything you demonstrated yourselves to be innocent in the matter" (2 Corinthians 7:11). People see you now, he says, and they know that you do not commit those sins that you used to. You have demonstrated yourself to be innocent; therefore your present actions vindicate any past wrongdoing.

HUMBLING OURSELVES

I know people whose pasts were awful. They could feel wretched over their former lives, and that could hinder their zeal, longing, and freshness for God, but it does not. Their present lives tell other people who continue to link those kinds of sins to them that those sins are in the past. Whenever the Holy Spirit convicts us, He expects us to humble ourselves. The forgiveness is already there, for God never allows us to be convicted without His forgiveness at hand. If that were not true, then the conviction itself would be nothing more than total condemnation. What is the good of being told you are wrong without any way to make things right or to be set free from sin's binding power?

Two individuals in the Bible demonstrate remorse but not repentance. One is Cain, who killed his brother Abel. Cain was full of sorrow for killing Abel. He even exclaimed, "My punishment is too great to bear!" (Genesis 4:13). However, all he was experiencing was condemnation. He was sorrowful, but not to the point of repentance, because rebellion was still in his heart. The other person is Judas. I have known many people who have tried somehow to get Judas into heaven. They believe that he got unfair treatment and that he should have made it. The point is that Judas did feel awful for betraying our Lord. He felt extreme remorse. Even the text says, "Judas, who had betrayed Him . . . felt remorse . . ." (Matthew 27:3). His attitude of rebellion continued, though, as he threw the money on the temple floor and out of disgust went out and killed himself. Did Judas repent? No. He never came to Christ to be set free. He never humbled himself before his Master. Throughout the Gospels one gets the impression that the one who would betray Jesus would be Peter. We know from history that it was Judas, but Peter was the one who stumbled so often. Judas betrayed the Lord in front of grown men. Peter denied the Lord in front of a girl, yet Peter came to grips with his sin. It was the same sin as Judas's, but Peter repented. Judas just felt condemned. Peter, through it all, was set free beyond words. He never made an issue of his betrayal afterwards. He was free from it, and far be it from him to keep bringing the matter up. If God had forgotten it, Peter had better, also. It is amazing that Jesus asked Peter about his love for Him three times, and yet He never mentioned Peter's betrayal. It was forgiven and forgotten. Jesus was interested only in "What now?" not "What about then?"

The rich man in Luke 18:23 went away "very sad" but not forgiven. He continued to carry his guilt and despair, whereas Paul is a beautiful example of a forgiven man. In

First Timothy 1:15, where he speaks of his horrendous actions before conversion (and we know from background material that they were horrendous), all he says is that he was chief of sinners. Paul could have gone into all sorts of things that God had forgiven him for, but what was the need? His position had changed, and he saw no reason to dig up what had been buried.

> *The only thing*
> *maturity adds is*
> *strength, not perfection.*

Basically, remorseful people do three things in contrast to repentant people. First, they constantly blame others for their failures. (As long as a person blames one other person for any failure, he has not truly repented.) Having never really given up their right to themselves, they still believe someone else should take part of the blame. Second, they constantly bring up their failures over and over again. One cannot talk to them for more than a few minutes without their past failures being talked about. Third, they quite often brag about their failures. They will say things like, "I am nothing; I cannot help for I have failed in the same area." There is a lot of pious pride in the insistence on being "nothing." People should just get on with what the Word of God teaches. If this is you, quit saying things about yourself that God's testimony of us does not say. If God has forgiven you, walk like a forgiven man. Nothing will thrill the Lord more than knowing that you believe you are clean as He says you are.

It is interesting to note in the Gospels that whomever

our Lord touched became whole. In every instance, even when just healing a hand, the text says that the person become "whole." Jesus loves to make things whole. Normally, when a baby is born, it has all of its parts. You would think it very strange if you were called over to someone's house to see the baby sprout fingers. No, babies are born with all their parts. The only thing growth adds is strength to those existing parts. Our position in Christ is like that. When we are born in Christ, we have all of our parts. We are as complete as we will get. The only thing maturity adds is strength, not perfection. A married person cannot be more married. We are all either married or unmarried. A person is either in Christ, or he is not. We cannot become more in Christ. God does not have special saints and unspecial ones. We are all complete at the time we repent and humble ourselves before the cross of Christ.

In Luke 10 we have the account of the seventy's going out to witness for the Lord. They came back rejoicing in the many experiences they had encountered. They had even cast demons out of others. As they became more and more excited, Jesus did not seem to be joining in with them. Instead, He told them that, if they were going to rejoice over experiences, He had reason to rejoice more than all of them. "I was watching Satan fall from heaven like lightning. . . . Nevertheless, do not rejoice in this, that the spirits are subject to you, but rejoice that your names are recorded in heaven" (Luke 10:18–20). Jesus is telling us to rejoice in who we are, not in what we do. Rejoice in your position, not necessarily in your practice. Your practice can change, your position cannot. Know your position. Any football coach will tell his players that as he works with the team. "Know your position," a coach will yell. When we all learn and practice our position, then we can work as a team for God's glory.

Nobody spent more time clarifying the doctrine of our position in Christ than did the apostle Paul. In fact, he pens the phrase "in Christ" 130 times in the thirteen epistles that he wrote. He used that phrase more than any other, knowing both its importance and the problem Christians would have if they were shaky on the subject. His two greatest chapters on the doctrine are Colossians 2 and Ephesians 1, both being inexhaustible in content. Let us look at those passages.

"For in Him all the fullness of Deity dwells in bodily form, and in Him you have been made complete" (Colossians 2:9–10). First, our position before God is one of *completeness*. We are complete. Literally, the verse means that "you have nothing less than Him." We have been made full; no additions are necessary. Christ affirmed that when on the cross He said, "It is finished!" His work is complete, and we are complete in Him. What a revelation! We are as complete as Christ. We are made whole, full, and complete. Nothing can be added to our salvation, not even our good intentions and works.

Second, not only are we complete, but the text goes on to say we are *circumcised*. "And in Him you were also circumcised with a circumcision made without hands, in the removal of the body of the flesh by the circumcision of Christ" (Colossians 2:11). The very context of that word *circumcision* implies that it is the nature of man that is being dealt with—the thing that passes sin from father to son. That nature had to be dealt with. When we become Christians, we do not just get whitewashed, we become totally new. He gives you a completely new nature. When we get to heaven, we are going to get a new body, not a new nature—we have that already.

Romans 7 compares our situation to that of a woman whose husband has died. She is set free from the marriage completely. It calls the old nature "crucified." Do not play with words here. To be crucified means just that—to be killed, to be put to death. "With my mind [I] am serving the law of God, but on the other [hand], with my flesh the law of sin" (Romans 7:25). "Our old self was crucified with Him, that our body of sin might be done away with" (Romans 6:6). The body of sin was not slightly altered, but "done away with," in a past tense experience. Claim it, rest in it, enjoy it, and thank God for it.

Are we free from ever sinning again? No, but we are free from sin's consequence, eternal death. The Bible says the "wages of sin is death" (Romans 6:23). How many times can sin kill us? If we are Christians we have already "died." Sin can kill us only once; therefore, when the devil comes to condemn us, we can tell him that sin has no claim on us. The penalty is death; we can only die once, and we have already died in Christ. All physical death really means to the Christian is getting rid of the problem of the flesh. There is no way to be made anew in Christ and go on as we have in the past. The flesh will still give us trouble, but God's law of liberty has set us free.

Not only are we complete and circumcised in Christ, but, third, we are *created anew* in Christ. "Having been buried with Him in baptism, in which you were also raised up with Him. . . . And when you were dead in your transgressions and the uncircumcision of your flesh, He made you alive together with Him" (Colossians 2:12–13a). What glory! All of our sins are forgiven. "Having forgiven us *all* our transgressions" (2:13b, italics added). We are a brand new creation from God.

When I am in meetings I often ask how many people believe that God has forgiven them of all their sins. The Christians all raise their hands. I go on to ask if they believe that God has even forgiven the sins they have not committed yet? They agree. Well, if God has forgiven the sins I have not even committed, then why ask forgiveness? You see, there is no such thing as an unforgiven sin in the life of a Christian. All sins are forgiven—past, present, and future. Then, I repeat, why ask forgiveness? The answer is to have your joy restored. A close study of 1 John 1 and Psalm 51 will reveal that we are to ask forgiveness in order to have our joy made full.

Our sins cannot change our relationship. "As far as the east is from the west, so far has He removed our transgressions" (Psalm 103:12). Notice the statement is "as far as the east is from the west," not "the north from the south." The latter are fixed points even though they are far away. The former are infinite directions. "I will not remember your sins" (Isaiah 43:25). "Blessed is he whose transgression is forgiven" (Psalm 32:1).

I believe that the highest judge in the universe is God. If God has forgiven me, then the only reason I could believe that I was not clean would be if I have a higher authority than God. I must humble myself to receive that forgiveness. Many people ask me what would happen to them as Christians, if they were to die with unconfessed sin. The very asking of the question shows the need for understanding of our position in Christ.

Fourth, Colossians 2 tells us that we are *cleansed.* "[He] canceled out the certificate of debt" (v. 14). Our sins piled up a debt before God. They were held against us. Colossians 2:14 says that God took the debt away and wiped the slate clean. We had asigned confession of debt that we owed. The "handwriting" was against us.

"When He had disarmed the rulers and authorities, He made a public display of them, having triumphed over them through Him" (Colossians 2:15). God took the entire debt we owed and nailed it to the cross. When the devil comes to condemn or accuse, take him to the cross. Did he find any fault in Jesus? No, and you are both complete and completely forgiven in Christ. Your debts of sin are nailed right there to the cross. Look at them. They are no longer yours, so they cannot bother you. The verse also tells us that God took the rulers and authorities and made a public display of them. The idea here is that of a wrestling match. You have seen tag team wrestling. When one fellow is being beaten he touches his partner, who comes in fresh to beat up on the fellow beating up his partner. That is what has happened to us. When we were down with the weight of Satan's accusations, Jesus reached out His hand, and we touched His. With one touch of His nail-scarred hand, He made a fool of the devil. He came into the ring and threw him off of us, publicly triumphing over him for the world to see. In other words, God ruined the devil's party. Satan was having a good time with us, and God put an end to it. The devil today continues to keep Christians spiritually beaten down by their insistence on being sin conscious. God is saying, "You're free. Now get on with it." We now owe a debt of thanksgiving and love. What higher motives for serving the Lord are there?

I have heard people saying, "I would love to begin the Christian life over again with present-tense knowledge." You can! Christianity is the only religion that allows it. Every moment God sees my sin as if it were the first time I had ever committed it. He does not remember when the last sin was. It is forgiven and forgotten. Why would you continue to bring up what God has dumped forever?

Prayer: O Lord, help me to comprehend Your testimony concerning me. What a complete work You have done. You died on my cross. I am now free to serve You out of love and thanksgiving. I am thankful, O Lord. I humble myself before

You. Keep me from being past conscious, sin conscious, or even self-conscious. I now find my security in You alone. My position in You is more than I can understand fully, but to the degree in which I do, I am overwhelmed. Thank You. Thank You.

9

ORDINARY ME WITH AN EXTRAORDINARY LOVE

One of the most beautiful love stories in the Bible is the story related in Ephesians 1. That chapter is filled with spiritual meat and with meaning for developing an extraordinary love relationship with the Lord. A brief spot check of the message in Ephesians will help us appreciate that love story.

Ephesians has two main sections—the first concerns doctrine; the second, duty. Duty is always the obvious response to doctrine; therefore, our practice in the Christian life must be based on a solid doctrinal position. Teaching only duty without doctrine weakens the counsel of God for the believer. It either leads to a legalistic spirit or causes the believer to try to live on emotional pep talks. If a Christian fails to conform to the pattern of the Bible, it is not because he lacks rules; it is because he lacks love. A person cannot look into the doctrine of our position in Christ without feeling that he owes a debt of love. Are we indebted? Surely! But not to rules. Instead our indebtedness is to love.

The story of the captain of a Mississippi riverboat illustrates that debt of love. As his ship went by another vessel, the captain grabbed a man and said, "Look, look over there at that captain."

The bystander wondered why he was so excited. He asked, "Why do you want me to look at that captain?"

Then the captain told him the story of how he had collided in the middle of the night with another boat several years before. The vessel was lost, and in the process he was thrown overboard. About that time, the other captain they had seen came by and jumped in to save his life. He looked at the bystander and said, "Ever since then I just love to point him out!" That is a perfect representation of the Christian life. The duty has vanished in light of the desire to "point Him out." We have been rescued, saved, secured, and loved. Now, we just love to point out the One who did it all.

RICHES OF THE BELIEVER

Ephesians 1:18–19 give us Paul's prayer for every Christian, which is consistent throughout his epistles. He always prays that the church will know her position in Christ and the riches obtained through that position. Paul prays that believers will be *enlightened:* "I pray that the eyes of your heart may be enlightened"; he prays that the church will be *encouraged:* "so that you may know what is the hope of His calling"; he prays that the church will be *enriched:* "what are the riches of the glory of His inheritance in the saints"; and he prays they will be *empowered:* "and what is the surpassing greatness of His power toward us who believe."

Ephesians stretches from eternity to eternity. Chapter 1 contains the longest sentence in the Bible. Ephesians 1:3–14 has no period. The passage contains 273 words in the Eng-

lish Bible, although grammarians tell us that a sentence
more than 30 words long is not good grammar. But where
would you put a period? You see, Paul knew his position in
Christ. He knew what he had in Christ and what a difference that made in his daily walk. He loved to flaunt the
riches he had in Christ. That is why he tells us in Ephesians
6 to "stand" when we are face to face with spiritual warfare.
We are already rich. Stand, therefore, on those riches. Don't
just appreciate them. Appropriate them!

All of God's riches and possessions are ours.

Note the teaching of chapters 1 and 2 concerning the believer: we are chosen (1:4), sanctified (1:4), adopted (1:5),
accepted (1:5), redeemed (1:7), forgiven (1:7), enriched
(1:8), enlightened (1:9), sealed (1:13), quickened (2:5), exalted (2:6), consecrated (2:10), reconciled (2:16), and united
(2:21). According to chapter 1, verse 4, we are filled with
purpose. We have been chosen by God for Himself out of the
world. Verses 5 and 6 tell us we have *prospect.* We have an
anticipation, a new outlook, and a foretaste. Verses 7 and 8
tell us we have *pardon.* Verses 9 and 10 tell us we have *power.*
Verse 11 tells us we have *plenty.* We have obtained an inheritance. All of God's riches and possessions are ours—no less
ours than His. Verses 13 and 14 tell us we have *peace.* We are
His; that means ownership. We are safe; that means security.
Then, to top it all off, we are *prayed* for by the Holy Spirit
Himself, who penned the prayer in verses 18 and 19.

That is the message and matchlessness of our position in
Christ. However, what exactly does it all mean to us? How

are we to respond to it? One might say, "I'm so ordinary! I'm so afraid of going after any truth and then not living it—with the result that I increase my guilt all the more."

There once was a girl who lived in a big city. She decided to go to college in a small town where the school was the only thing there. She was quite unattached and acted as though she would be single forever. The moment she stepped onto the campus of the college, she heard about a man who was supposed to be the "greatest guy in the world." She ignored the talk. Certainly, she figured, no man was that great.

Weeks went by and she still heard of his being so fantastic. Everywhere she went she heard about the fellow—in the laundromat, in grocery stores, and especially among the girls on campus. After several months she told the other girls, "Your problem is that you so seldom see any good-looking guys in this hick town that you go bananas when you see one!"

The talk, however, went on and on. After about six months, she was studying for exams when the phone rang. She picked it up, and guess who was on the other end? No, you are wrong. It was the father of the fellow about whom she had heard so much. He said, "Sally?"

"Yes, this is Sally."

"Well, I am the father of 'so and so.'"

"Oh, I have heard a lot about your son."

"I trust it was good."

"Oh, yes, too good. I doubt anybody could be quite as great as what I have heard!"

"Well, the reason I have called is to tell you that I have chosen you to be the wife of my son."

"What? Oh, no, you don't. I have promised myself never to marry any person I have not met!"

"I can understand that. He will be over to pick you up for a date at seven thirty."

"Well, I can't be ready in four hours."

"I'm sorry, but you must be ready at seven thirty."

When she hung up the telephone, she immediately called all the girls to tell them what had happened.

Finally, the moment came. He was there at 7:30, and they had their date. She came home so dumbfounded that she just lay across the bed and cried. "How could anybody be so amazing?" she asked herself. "He was ten times greater than anyone told me. I thought for sure he would be a letdown, but he was like no one I have ever known."

The relationship progressed until one day he popped the big question. "Sally, will you marry me?"

"Yes, yes, yes!"

Everything had happened so quickly, and she found herself so wrapped up in their relationship that Sally quite forgot about her past. Suddenly, she remembered that this man was too great for her to bring all of her past debts into the marriage. You see, she had been quite a "swinger." She had bought a new Jaguar for $35,000 and still owed a large balance. She had bought $15,000 worth of furniture for her apartment and clothes. She had purchased $5,000 worth of jewelry from Tiffany's. She was really in debt. How could she drag that debt into the marriage? She could not even bear the thought of telling the fellow about it. She decided to go to each place of indebtedness and work out a plan, even if it meant giving back what she bought.

She went to the Jaguar business office and told them that she was marrying a fantastic guy and could not drag her debts into their marriage. She said, "I am even ready to give up the car. What can I do? This guy is too great for me to abuse him with my debts."

The office manager told her, "You haven't heard?"

"I haven't heard what?"

"Well, just before you came in, a guy was in here and paid your debt in full."

"What?! You mean—"

"Yes! It is all paid for." She staggered out of the office, then ran back in. "What did he look like?"

"He had dark hair, blue eyes, and a nice smile."

"*That's him!* That's the guy I'm marrying!"

She drove her Jaguar to the business office of the department store where she had bought her furniture and clothes. She went in and said, "I am marrying this great guy. I know I have debts with you, but as time goes by, this guy gets better and better. I can't bear the thought of dragging these debts into our marriage. What can I work out with you?"

The office manager looked at her with surprise. "You haven't heard?" he shouted! "Just a few moments ago a guy came in and paid the entire debt. You are free from any more payments."

"You must be kidding me!"

"No."

"What did this guy look like?"

"He had dark hair, blue eyes, and a smile like—"

"*That's him!* That's him! That's the one I'm marrying!"

She got into her car and zoomed over to Tiffany's. Her mind was "blown away" with all of this. She staggered into the office and asked to see the manager. She began to explain, "I am marrying this great guy, and I can't drag this five thousand dollar debt into our marriage. I believe I have the money now to pay it all off. What do I owe?"

The office manager looked at her like the others had. "You don't know?"

She said, "You have to be kidding me!"

"No, a fellow just came in. I don't know how you missed him. He paid it in full."

"Oh, *wow!*" she exclaimed.

On the way to her apartment she began to cry. She wept because she felt so unworthy, and yet so special, for being the bride-to-be of such a man.

She ran into the house to call him. When he answered, she said, "Thank you, thank you, thank you. Everywhere I went today you had been before me. You knew about my debts and met every need. Thank you, thank you, thank you."

"Oh, you are welcome," he said. "Are you going to be free tonight? . . . Good, I will be over at seven."

The relationship continued until the wedding day was drawing near. She decided to go to Fifth Avenue in New York to buy the gown of the decade. She had the money now to buy the one she had always wanted—a wedding gown with gorgeous lace and a ten-foot train. She went to the cashier to pay and said, "What do I owe on this gown?"

The cashier looked at her and said, "You haven't heard? Just before you came in, a guy came by and said, 'Anything my bride wants to make our marriage the best, you give it to her.' Your wedding gown is paid for already. This must be some man you are marrying," the cashier said.

"Oh, I wish you could really get to know him. He is great!"

Let us pause for a moment with the parable. That is the message of Ephesians 1. God the Father has called us to be the bride of His Son. Not only did Christ ask us to be His very own, but He also took out of the way all the hindrances to our being a good bride. With one move of His nail-scarred hand, He wiped clean all the debts that we had incurred. He lavished upon us His riches and forgiveness in order for us to be a perfect and unblemished bride (Ephesians 1:7–8).

The wedding day came, and finally they were married. What a union it was! Sally's entire motivation was the love of a thankful girl for a great husband. She had only one desire: never to hurt her husband in any way, but just to love him. At times she did hurt him, and he would just love her in return. She felt bad for doing it, but she was free to fail around this great husband.

> ### The highest motive for obedience is love resulting from gratitude.

She would often look at the ring he had given her, especially when he had to be away for long periods of time. She would view the ring as the seal of their marriage. It comforted her in her loneliness to know that he had given her a seal signifying the statement "I do."

Christian, we have been given a seal of God's commitment to us. It is the Holy Spirit. He is the pledge of what is to come and of the fact that we belong to God.

When I am gone from home, the ring my wife has given me is not for my sake, necessarily. It is for those who see me. Others could ask, "I wonder if Dan DeHaan is married?" Then they could look at the ring on my finger and see that I am. They know that I belong to someone. It is an amazing fact that the moment I said, "I do," to my wife it meant that I said, "I don't," to 110 million other women in America. Before then, I always wondered, "Is it her, Lord, or is it her?" But the moment I was ready to say, "I do," I knew my wife was the one.

When we became Christians, God not only forgave us and forgot all of our sins and debts, but then He sealed our union with Himself with the mark indicating that we had better be left alone; we are His very own property.

Let me ask you a question. What do you believe was Sally's motive in being a good wife to her husband? You know it had to be love and thankfulness. She was so full of love for her freedom and full of thankfulness for her forgiveness that she made an excellent wife. Some have told me that an understanding of our position in Christ gives us a license to go on sinning. If it does, then you know nothing of what I just said. The highest motive in the world and in heaven for obedience is love resulting from gratitude. If a man gave you a million dollars today, you would not spit in his face. You would say, "What can I do for you? Can I clean your yard, wash your car, help you in any way?" That is the only response that will pass the test of our motives, by which we will all be judged (1 Corinthians 4:5).

Are you in love with the Lord? Could you say that the reason you do what you do is because you are in love with the Lord? Do you get up and have a quiet time, or do you just arise and love the Lord? One can be rote, whereas the other is always fresh. Do you ever do anything spontaneously just to show the Lord that you love Him?

To develop that love relationship takes sitting down with Him often just to share yourself. How much time you spend with someone is often an indication that you love him. All true love involves sacrifice. When God speaks to us, He might ask us to stop something that previously was not wrong to us. Do we argue about it, or give it up? Is He so cheap that we offer Him little or nothing? Real love motivates and makes us sensitive to the person we are loving. Real love makes us full of gratitude!

I often picture Paul in jail expressing his thanks to God and God's responding to Paul. Paul was so in love with the Lord—so sensitive to what God wanted. He pleased God by being so thankful for even the little things. Paul would say thank You to the Lord for being all He was to Paul. Do you ever wonder why Paul was so motivated and thankful all the time? It had to do with his humility before God. He honestly believed that he deserved nothing and, therefore, anything was a blessing. Our problem many times is that we think we deserve so much. Until God does something bigger than what we think we deserve, we complain. All murmuring and grumbling is a sign of the lack of motivation, love, and thankfulness. Oh, Christian, let God break your heart, even now, for your lack of yielded love—for your lack of weeping before Him for all He has done for you.

Solomon asks the question, "What kind of beloved is your beloved?" (Song of Solomon 5:9). Paul knew the answer and lived the answer to the full. Paul found himself with new *liberty* (Galatians 5:1, 13); new *life* (Colossians 3:3; 1:27); new *law* (Romans 7:23–25); new *light* (1 Corinthians 4:5); new *laughter* (Philippians 3:1); new motivation in *labor* (1 Corinthians 15:58); new *leader* (Colossians 1:18); new *lips* (Colossians 3:8, 17); new *loss* (Philippians 3:7–8, he lost what he didn't need to gain—what was indispensible); new *look* (2 Corinthians 4:18); new *love* (2 Corinthians 5:14); and he certainly got a new *lord* (Philippians 3:8). He spent the rest of his life saying, *"Thank You, Lord!"*

Would your family say that your life is characterized by a thankful heart? Would others around you say that you are filled with a love for the Lord? Many, I have found, have obedience according to their rules for the Lord. They do not always have a love for the Lord. They view God as a great teacher, so they become a great student—determined to get straight A s. They view God as primarily holy, so they walk the straight and narrow for fear that God's wrath will come. God is a Father and He has given us all things and we are to love Him as only we can. No other part of creation can do that.

If a sign were hung around your neck that said, "What I

do for the Lord is wholly because I love Him!" would what it said be true?

Prayer: Lord, my heart is so full of grateful praise. Oh, what a wondrous privilege to be Your bride—to be clothed in Your righteousness—to be the recipient of all Your favor and grace. Forgive my heart for its pride in being demanding of You. Forgive me for my lack of sensitivity to what You have already done. Forgive me, O God, for my lack of love. My heart sobs for its hardness toward such a gracious, giving God. I allow it to break for Your glory. Mend it back to say as Paul did, "The love of Christ controls me."*

* 2 Corinthians 5:14.

10
BALANCING THE CHRISTIAN LIFE (PART 1)

Many individuals today are highly qualified to be utterly useless. They have trained themselves to be proficient in a few areas, approaching their ministry like a specialist in a large corporation. God makes clear in His Word that He does not anoint gifts or talents, but men. God is looking for men who know Him well, fear apathy supremely, and hate sin immensely.

God is looking for leaders. Today there is a dire need for leaders in the church. As Leonard Ravenhill says so clearly in his book *America Is Too Young to Die*, this is a nation in need of prophets. We need men who do not define balance in the Christian life as having time every day for physical exercise, but who define it as consistent love, loyalty, and leadership for God's glory.

Having looked at the concept of God that He desires us to have and having seen our position in Christ, we must now put it all together and see the balanced Christian life. It is that balance that produces men who do not just perform but who have a passion for God. It is that balance that makes a man see his M.Q. (Motivation Quotient) as more important than his I.Q., and that made Paul so faithful, forceful, and fearless. The church today has gone from one side of the evangelical pendulum to the other, having searched out every way to compete with the world and influence its territory.

We have worn ourselves out serving the One who said, "My yoke is easy and My burden is light." The Christian life is not that complicated. Let us find the balance and then get on with it. Peter's statement in Luke 5 is classic. "Master, we worked hard all night and caught nothing" (v. 5). We should know by now that anything that begins with "we" will end with "nothing." The purpose of this book is to impress you with the God that we serve. How should we respond to our God? We should put into practice our love, our position in Christ, and our knowledge of God's character. We should train our senses to discern good and evil (Hebrews 5:14). "Only conduct yourselves in a manner worthy of the gospel of Christ" (Philippians 1:27). How, then, does our response fit in with the balanced Christian life?

In my mind, no person is better qualified to teach us about balance than the apostle Paul, and he does so in the book of Philippians. That book was written to ground the few believers at Philippi in the balanced Christian life. At age sixty-two he tells them of his life. Paul needed balancing as we do. He had to learn the difference between a spirit-anointed man and a gifted leader. He was both, but the latter had to give way to the former.

OUR POSSESSION

Philippians has four chapters that divide into four parts. A balanced Christian life can be found by utilizing each of these four parts. The first chapter of Philippians tells us that Christ must be our *possession*. In chapter 1 the key phrase is "in Christ." Remember, it is that phrase that Paul used 130 times in his thirteen epistles. The key verse is verse 6, "For I am confident of this very thing, that He who began a good work in you will perfect it until the day of Christ Jesus." The result of having Christ as your possession will always be *confidence*.

It used to bother me that Paul would say to imitate him (1 Corinthians 4:16). I wondered if with such an ego he were qualified to be the model Christian. Then I discovered that the reason for his indomitable will and confidence was because he knew he was "in Christ" and he knew what that meant on the street, in jail, or in a mansion. The first chapter of Ephesians clearly conveys the position Paul saw that he had and the confidence that resulted.

Lack of confidence is a spiritual problem. There are a few evangelical extroverts around who are naturally confident; however, their natural gift often gets in the way of God's supernatural supply. Confidence is a direct result of knowing your position in Christ. Notice the references to confidence in Philippians, chapter 1 (italics added). "I want you to *know,* brethren . . ." (v. 12); "For I *know* that this shall turn out for my deliverance . . ." (v. 19); "According to my earnest *expectation and hope, that I shall not be put to shame in anything,* but that with all *boldness* . . ." (v. 20); "And *convinced* of this, *I know* that I shall remain and continue" (v. 25); "So that your proud *confidence* in me may abound" (v. 26)—Paul is saying in verse 26 that his confidence will generate their confidence; seeing his contentment in jail encouraged their confidence in whatever situation they found themselves; "In *no way alarmed* by your opponents . . ." (v. 28).

All of chapter 1 focuses on the result of being in Christ, that is, *confidence.* In Mark 4:35–41 we have the account of the disciples in "rough water." There was a storm sent by God to examine their confidence in Christ. Jesus was asleep on a cushion. Note the restfulness and confidence He had, as opposed to the disciples who were more afraid for their own lives. They asked, "Teacher, do You not care that we are perishing?" Jesus, after calming the storm with three words, said to them, "Why are you so timid? How is it that you have no faith?" The *you* here is in the emphatic tense, meaning "you, of all people." Jesus was in effect saying, "You are My disciples. Why do you act as though events take place without My approval or without My knowing it?" If you are secure in your position in Christ, that will always produce calmness in the midst of calamity.

*Jesus did not come
to make bad men good,
but to make dead men live.*

Isaiah 32:17 gives great light on this subject. "And the work of righteousness will be peace, and the service of righteousness, quietness and *confidence forever*" (italics added). Righteousness produces confidence. Knowing our position in Christ, which is both complete and perfect, will produce confidence. That brings up a grave problem in the church today. Confidence is needed in the area of leadership. God is looking for men who, when they meet together, pray with confidence, communicate with confidence, and trust Him with confidence.

The problem is that many men in leadership are unholy men. Some have no position in Christ—they are unsaved.

Church discipline is almost unheard of. As one pastor confessed to me, "Where would we begin?" The doctrine of our position in Christ can never produce comfortableness, as we see in so much of the church. Instead, knowing our position in Christ produces a consistent confidence that what God said is true, as well as a determination to work out what God has shown us. Ephesians tells us that lack of unity, lack of intensity, and lack of authority reveal a lack of our being "in Christ" (Ephesians 4–6). If we were to raise the qualifications for membership in local churches, and especially for their leadership, we would find fewer men, but greater power.

Jesus did not come to make bad men good, but to make dead men live. The church should demand that men be alive in Christ, opposed to being simply good. What is a Christian? He is an ordinary person with an extraordinary love. A love that consistently "lays ourselves down" for the sake of seeing God exalted. It is love that motivates us, that clings to nothing that God gives save Himself. So many today have a "handle" on the ministry when the ministry should have a handle on them.

Are you in Christ? Is there a definite divine motivation and confidence in your soul? Are you really in love with the Lord Himself? Can you honestly say that the experience you have had with Christ has made you alive and not just good? If you cannot, I would ask that God would break your heart even now—that, first, you would see your sin; that, second, you would see the righteousness and blood of the Lamb that can cleanse it all; and that, third, you would cast your sin and self on the cross of Christ. Then your old nature will be crucified, and you will join those who have their confidence in Christ, not those who have only a knowledge of how to work for Him.

OUR PATTERN

The second part of the balanced Christian life is found in Philippians 2. Whereas Philippians 1 has told us that Christ must be our *possession,* the second chapter says that Christ must be our *pattern.* The key phrase in that chapter is "like Christ." The key verses are verses 3–7. The result of having Christ as our pattern will always be *humility.* Philippians 2 is the greatest chapter in the Bible on the humiliation of Jesus Christ, and it serves as the pattern for the believer. Notice how that fits in with the earlier chapters of the book. We can be sure that we are alive in Christ, and therefore have a confidence that ignites our motivation. Is that a balanced Christian life? No! It is not enough just to be confident. The balanced life must begin there, but confidence without humility can lead to presumption. We see that Paul goes on to talk on the second part of the Christian life, continuing to remain Christ-centered in all of his emphasis. The Christian life is Christ living through a man, not a man trying to be Christ.

People have some gross misconceptions of what humility is. Men can be so pious in their conversations that others believe they are humble, but that is not humility at all. It is an example of the art of manipulation, leading to the art of intimidation. True humility is unconscious servanthood. It is a willingness to be ruled without having to concentrate on being submissive. It demands that we have "kicked out" of us a consciousness that we are humble.

Sometimes after meetings leaders will ask how to handle compliments. They struggle with the problem, feeling that they must go off and confess the sin of pride when they receive compliments. The very fact that they are having to deal with receiving compliments indicates that they are proud men. The most humble among us is like Christ; you

could flatter Him or flatten Him, but His attitude and actions would not change. Humility is the great gift from God
that keeps a man true and faithful when he has received a
blessing or when he has received a blow.

We lose our anointing as men of God when we begin to
concentrate on what God has told us to give up—that is,
ourselves. A man once asked if it would be all right for him
to have the goal of being like Christ. It sounded good at
first, but I replied, "Well, what would that mean to you if
you accomplished your goal?"

He immediately went on to tell me all the things he
could do: "I could discern men's thoughts; I could counsel
better; I could preach while keeping people spellbound; I
could be used to do mighty things for God . . ." He used the
personal pronoun *I* about twenty times in a few seconds.
Needless to say, it would be wrong for him to have that goal.
His idea of the goal to be like Christ was far from God's idea.
Increased humility is a decrease of the "I" in life. Humility
just "gets on with it" for God's glory. It does not consider the
type of job or amount of prestige. I am to humble myself,
and God will exalt in due time.

There is no rebellion whatsoever in the life of one who is
truly humble. Jesus taught us that when He said, "My food
is to do the will of Him who sent Me" (John 4:34), and, "Not
as I will, but as Thou wilt" (Matthew 26:39).

Every time we think we have Jesus "pegged," He goes
against the grain of how we understand humility. For instance, the Sermon on the Mount speaks of humility and
the turning of the "other cheek," yet we see Jesus angry at
sin in the temple (Matthew 21:12). Humility is always out
to protect what is right, and it is always concerned with
another's welfare—in that case, God's. Humility will allow
itself to be slandered, but it cannot tolerate God's name to
be slandered. It can receive a compliment and without

conscious effort know the compliment is sent from and returned to God. I cannot become more like Christ than when I am in a position of having all that glorifies me laid down. Humility is seen in a person living for the Lord completely and unconsciously. What a joy to see a person happy for no earthly reason; that takes humility.

What is your point of pride? Is there unconscious pride in your life with Christ? Do you find yourself easily broken before Him? Are *His* interests the major reason for your anger when they are violated? Are His interests the major reason for your joy when they are pursued? Or are your anger and joy coming from what you accomplish, receive, and get out of your own determined effort? Understanding humility is a major step in the Christian life. Only God can work it in a person.

A person who is selfish has little capacity to love.

Our high position in Christ demands a lowly walk. Two phrases from Philippians 2 illustrate humility. The first is "emptied Himself" (2:7); the second is "being poured out" (2:17). Humility is emptying oneself or pouring oneself out. It is interesting to note that chapter 2 records the humble attitude of four different people—Jesus emptied Himself (2:7); Paul poured himself out (2:17); Timothy did not seek after his own interests (2:21); and Epaphroditus risked his life for others (2:30). Those men taught that humility is a part of the balanced Christian life.

The deadliest sins are conquered by the great attitude of humility. Chapter 2 lists all five "deadly sins" as though the antidote for them is humility. The first sin listed is *apathy* (2:2, 4, 8, 12, 16). Notice a few of the verses making a direct attack against it (italics added)—"Make my joy complete by being of the same mind . . . *intent on one purpose*" (v. 2). "He humbled Himself by becoming *obedient to the point of death,* even death on a cross" (v. 8). "*Work out* your salvation *with fear and trembling*" (v. 12). "Because *I did not run in vain nor toil in vain*" (v. 16). Those verses all reveal apathy's being put away. That deadly sin creeps into a church or a youth group, and just like a cancer it can destroy. We must stop it or it will stop us.

The second deadly sin, *selfishness,* is also found in Philippians 2 (vv. 4–6, 14). "Do not merely look out for your own personal interests, but also for the interests of others. . . . Do all things without grumbling or disputing." It takes an unselfish person not to murmur. If we are filled with pride, then it takes a lot to keep us satisfied. Everything, short of our personal pride's being satisfied, is murmured against. It is a terrible sin. A person who is selfish has little capacity to love. Everything he does is seen from the viewpoint of what will benefit his own selfish ego. Christ's pattern for us kicks right through the middle of that sin. Let us allow God to kick a hole through our selfishness.

Lack of quietness is the third deadly sin (2:5–6, 14). "Do all things without grumbling or disputing." The very nature of this chapter demands that we quiet ourselves often in humility before God. At this point we return to the importance of knowing God. His acquaintance is not made hurriedly. Many people, especially young people, cannot stay quiet for any length of time. They need to have things going on constantly, or they have to be with someone constantly. Quietness is next to insanity to many people. They are hooked on noise, and they cannot break the habit. What is the cure? Look to Christ. He knew how to enjoy the Father. He knew how to communicate with Him. If we follow Christ's pattern of humility, it becomes the promise of quietness in our heart and in our actions.

Lack of hatred for sin is mentioned as the fourth deadly sin (2:15, 30, italics added). "That you may *prove yourselves to be blameless and innocent,* children of God *above reproach* in the midst of a crooked and perverse generation, among whom you *appear as lights* in the world. . . . Because he *came close to death* for the work of Christ." When you identify yourself with God's interests, you begin to hate what He hates. We must not just have a dislike for sin. The world has that many times. It does not like what sin is doing to our country. But we must have God's view on sin. He hates it! Christ is the pattern. His death on the cross is proof of God's hatred of sin.

The fifth deadly sin is *pride* (2:21). "For they all seek after their own interests, not those of Christ Jesus." We have spent a great amount of time talking about that sin, so I will not take more time now. True humility is never piousness. It is a seeking after the things of God, as opposed to my own interests.

Epaphroditus gives us a great climax to balance in the Christian life. Philippians 2:30 says he risked his life. The Greek word for "risked" is a gambler's word, meaning that he gambled his life in reckless courage to serve Christ. He might lose his life, or he might make greater gains with it. In any case, he was willing to gamble for the results God would have. It is encouraging that humility is not just a practice we are to have today, but that it permeated the lives of many people like those we have seen in Philippians 2.

Christ must be our possession and then our pattern. The former produces confidence; the latter produces humility. At this point, we are 50 percent of what God wants us to be. The next chapter completes the last two areas that will enable us to have a balanced walk with God.

Prayer: Lord, I know what You want is my decision and commitment to empty myself. Choosing to keep myself in balance according to Your rules is where I need Your enabling. I long to be one who is being used as a leader among the sheep. I know what that will cost me! It will cost me my right to myself! I give up my selfishness and the deadly sins that make me immune to the desperate day I live in. Remind me when I am looking out for my own selfish interests rather than for those of the people I am leading. I would rather know Your daily judgment when I am out of balance spiritually than to find out such a great inconsistency in the last day. Lord, help me!

11

BALANCING THE CHRISTIAN LIFE (PART 2)

The apostle Paul tells us about the third part of the balanced Christian life in Philippians 3. Chapter 1 teaches that Christ must be our possession, chapter 2 that He must be our pattern. Now, we see that Christ must be our *purpose*. The key phrase in chapter three is "to know Christ." The key verse is verse 10—"That I may know Him. . . ." The result of having Christ as our purpose will be a life with direction, guidance, and motivation.

OUR PURPOSE

Chapter 3 is filled with purpose. One leaves the chapter consumed with Paul's divine motivation to live for the Lord. Let us look at a few verses showing that purpose in Paul's life (italics added). "But whatever things were gain to me, those things *I have counted as loss* for the sake of Christ" (v. 7). "*I count all things to be loss* in view of the surpassing *value of knowing Christ*" (v. 8). "But I press on in order *that I may lay* hold . . ." (v. 12). "*Forgetting* what lies behind and *reaching forward* to what lies ahead . . ." (v. 13). "*I press on toward the goal*" (v. 14). "Brethren, *join in following my example,* and observe those who walk according to the *pattern you have in us*" (v. 17). Those few verses gives us a spot check on the message of *purpose* in the Christian life.

There is a great need for purpose in the church. As in our great need for leadership, too many are followers and too few are initiators. We are too much like each other; we lack individuality. There is a lack of personal direction; therefore, we just follow any leader. We are not to become like each other; we are to become like Christ. There is room in Christ for amazing uniqueness, creativity, and individuality. He did not come to stereotype us but to give us life. What a joy to find a sixteen- or seventeen-year-old person who knows where he is going in life. He has not been enamored by the drifting age we live in. That kind of person will have an impact on America's great need for purpose and direction.

When I speak to youth and youth directors, this problem almost always arises. Low-level creativity hits the group, and people begin to lose interest for lack of direction. Where are our dreamers? Where are the men who can get alone with God for two hours and come out with three pages of creative ideas? Where are the "thus saith the Lord" men today? America is dying for lack of purpose. If the church does not fill this need, we had better admit defeat now. Hell and all its demons know exactly where they are going with this world, and God is looking for men who dare to match their intensity in purpose.

Philippians 3 brings us right back to the earlier chapters of this book. We are "to know Him." That is the basis of purpose in the Christian life. Whatever a person worships will determine the purpose he has in life. Let us be careful what we worship. Paul was very careful. He knew the difference between worshiping what will pass away and worshiping what will endure.

"Finally, my brethren, rejoice in the Lord" (3:1). Paul knew that apathy or lack of purpose will destroy a rejoicing Christian. We all know that boredom produces sadness, self-pity, and restlessness. Paul wants the church to know what it means to rejoice. I suppose he could have said, "Have a great time in the Lord," or, "Don't let lack of direction rob you of happiness," or even, "Experience the thrill of becoming all that God wants you to become." Those are the concerns of Paul's heart, and obviously of God's heart.

✳ *All worship involves sacrifice.*

"Beware of the dogs, beware of the evil workers, beware of the false circumcision" (3:2). Here is that statement that has been made famous on fences all over America—"Beware of dogs." Who are those dogs, evil workers, and false circumcisers? They are the legalists—those who would bind you with their lists of dos and don'ts. Paul says to beware of being bitten by a legalistic dog. They will rob you of your joy in the Lord. They will try to make you conform to a pattern instead of to a Person. They intimidate with their spiritual lists instead of inspiring with their spiritual lives. "The letter kills, but the Spirit gives life." (2 Corinthians 3:6). What is the antidote to legalism? It is keeping a rejoicing heart through having your eyes on the Lord and not on other people.

The true followers of Christ are those who "worship in the Spirit of God and glory in Christ Jesus and put no confidence in the flesh" (3:3). No man who worships Jesus Christ ever wants to be exalted. He becomes a man who knows where to put his confidence. He knows the weakness of human attainments. He knows the false pride of personal achievements. He knows how fast the balloon of self-trust can burst when punctured by God. The proof of Paul's attitude toward self-confidence is clear through the rest of the chapter. Verses 4 through 6 tell us about his human attainments and pride. Then he adds, "But whatever things were gain to me, those things I have counted as loss for the sake of Christ. More than that, I count all things to be loss in view of the surpassing value of knowing Christ Jesus my Lord . . . and count them but rubbish in order that I may gain Christ . . . not having a righteousness of my own derived from the Law" (3:7–9).

Do not complicate that set of verses. Paul is simply saying that all worship involves sacrifice. There is always gain and loss in the life of a rejoicing and balanced Christian. That is one way God keeps us from getting attached to what we should not. It is a way God keeps us from getting comfortable. "Present your bodies a living and holy sacrifice . . . which is your spiritual service of worship" (Romans 12:1). It is the reasonable thing to do—to give back to God both the good and the bad of our pasts. The good things can cause us to get satisfied, and the bad can fill our minds with guilt and despair. Leave them alone after they have been put on the cross of Christ. God wants you to have the same tastelessness that a newborn baby would have.

"Lay aside every encumbrance, . . . and let us run with endurance the race that is set before us" (Hebrews 12:1). The joy of winning a race is beyond words. The greater the race, the more intense the training, and as a result, the greater the joy in winning. The athlete has to put aside two basic patterns of thought: He must put behind him the good that was accomplished in the last race, if indeed there was good. And, he must put behind him the bad that was a result of the last race. Both could hinder every day's practice and ultimately the race itself.

The two most common methods of attack on the Christian's desire to have God's best are pride and despair, flattery and flattening. Paul's past was good by way of heritage, but he had to leave it alone. Pride over the past does not increase our present knowledge of God. "That I may know Him, and the power of His resurrection and the fellowship of His sufferings, being conformed to His death . . ." (3:10). Every part of that key verse implies intimacy. It is enough for most men to know the Lord, but Paul wanted to know the Lord and therefore wanted to know God's power, fellowship, and endurance. Did Paul know God in that way? Apparently he did. "I have fought the good fight, I have finished the course, I have kept the faith" (2 Timothy 4:7).

Paul's attitude was one of pressing on. "But I press on . . . and reaching forward . . . I press on toward the goal . . ." (3:12–14). "For consider Him who has endured such hostility by sinners against Himself, so that you may not grow weary and lose heart" (Hebrews 12:3). If we were not to press on, sin would entrap us; we would grow weary, lose heart, and quit. Some time ago my son Johnny said to me, "Dad, wouldn't it be terrible to have just quit the Christian life when the trumpet blows for God to call us home?" And what a tragedy it would be to live a life of apathy here and then miss the joy of having finished a race. Worship is the key action in the spiritual race, and the third chapter of Philippians will not let us escape it.

Verses 17–19 shed more light on the balance in the Christian's life. Paul refers to the opposite of worship: "That they are enemies of the cross of Christ, whose end is destruction, whose god is their appetite, and whose glory is in their shame,

THE GOD YOU CAN KNOW

who set their minds on earthly things" (3:18–19). Instead, we are to glory in the cross of Jesus Christ, because we had nothing to do with the result of that. God took the initiative to meet us where we were lacking. We owe a debt of thanksgiving and love. Who are the enemies of that cross? They are (1) those whose god is their appetite—those who lust after what is passing away, (2) those who glory in themselves—they will be put to shame one day when all is seen for what it really is, and (3) those who have set their minds on earthly things. "As [a man] thinks within himself, so he is" (Proverbs 23:7). If I set my mind on the earth, I am earthly. How foolish to gain what we cannot keep and lose what would have lasted forever. "For our citizenship is in heaven" (3:20). Earthbound saints offer little help to hell-bound sinners. This world is just not capable of changing people; God's world is.

What is your mind preoccupied with? Are you a worshiper of Jesus Christ? Would you say that you are a rejoicing Christian? Have you considered human attainments and past heritage loss for the sake of knowing Christ? Do you want to know Him beyond all other desires? That is what God desires. Only when you know Him will you endure through anything on earth. Only then will you rejoice when there is no earthly reason. Only then will you with Paul have run the good race and finished the course.

When I was a youth director, if an activity could be done and it was not sinful, we did it. One of those exciting events was what we called a "bigger and better hunt." I gave three separate groups a very small object. I would let them out in well-to-do neighborhoods about a mile apart and then let them have two hours to work on it. They would knock on doors and say, "We are on a bigger and better hunt and would like to trade this object for something bigger and better in your home." On one occasion the first group began with a pack of gum, another with a pen, and the last with some soap. After two hours I began to get concerned and tried to round the groups up. I honked the horn on the bus and finally the first group came down the road. You would not believe what they had traded up to from a pack of gum. Coming down the road toward me was a group of guys carrying a sofa. They had gone from one house to another, getting something bigger and better each time, and finally had traded up to a sofa. (By the way, the sofa was a very nice one that we were able to use in the youth building.)

The second group came back with a charcoal burner. It was the fancy kind that does a large cookout. The third group came back with a swinging pendulum clock, and it worked. After that day all they ever wanted to do was to go on "bigger and better hunts."

If you can imagine such a thing—God is forever on a bigger and better hunt. *He* has what is bigger and better and He comes knocking on our door. The more we grow, the more sensitive we become to His knocking and the better His gift becomes. However, there is one catch; it has to be a trade. He only gives us what is bigger and better when we make a trade from our smaller and worse. He is saying to every Christian over and over, "Will you trade what you have there for what is bigger and better? Will you give over to Me what you hold so dear?" Not until there is a trade does God give the greater.

The mark of a spiritually hungry man is right here. He knows God is continuously on a "bigger and better hunt" and is looking for people who will sacrifice what they cannot keep to gain what they cannot lose. Paul was well aware of that principle, but saints today seem ignorant of it. The Christian life is a continuous gain and loss. The loss seems less painful all the time because of the eternal gain being offered. To "finish the course" God will have to break your heart often over what you call so dear to yourself.

THE GOD YOU CAN KNOW

OUR POWER

Paul gives us the last part of the balance to the Christian life in chapter 4. We have seen that Christ must be our possession—that Christ must be our pattern—that Christ must be our purpose. Now, we come to see that Christ must be our *power*. The key phrase in this chapter is "through Christ." The key verse is verse 13. "I can do all things through Him [Christ] who strengthens me." The result of having Christ as our power will always be the strength to do all that is required of me.

As we come to this last part of our balance, it seems inconceivable that there would be more. It seems that if Christ were our possession, pattern, and purpose, then we would have our act together. No, Christ must be our power as well. The other parts of the balance are mere words that will condemn apart from God's power's enabling us to grasp, understand, and live them. Power in the Christian life is not given to make us act like super human beings. It is given to do in us what those in the "world" can never do for themselves.

The fourth chapter of Philippians spends a great deal of time on things like contentment, peace, and a clear mind. No seminar or book can make a man content. Notice the impossible statements in this chapter. "Rejoice in the Lord always; again I will say, rejoice! . . . Be anxious for nothing, but in everything by prayer and supplication with thanksgiving let your requests be made known to God. And the peace of God, which surpasses all comprehension, shall guard your hearts and your minds. . . . Whatever is honorable, whatever is right . . . let your mind dwell on these things" (vv. 4–8). Then Paul adds, "The things you have learned and received and heard and seen in me, practice these things" (4:9). How can we practice all of the things we have learned through Paul? Was Paul a "supersaint"? No,

Paul was an ordinary man with an extraordinary power given to him to live for Christ.

Paul closes the book of Philippians showing us the greatest power there is, that is the power to be content with whatever God gives you. Our self-life loves to complain, murmur, and argue. God's power can change all of that into a contentment that will baffle even the closest of friends. It is a wonderful thing to see a person with the power of God in his life. He says, "Thank you," for things we would not consider even mentioning. He gets excited over little things as well as big things, knowing that all things are given to him by God. He accepts what God gives him with open hands, and he leaves his hands open in case God would desire to take it away.

How about you? Are you known for your thankfulness? Would people say, "You just amaze me in how you consistently remain grateful and appreciative." Do you act and talk as though God never makes a mistake? That takes God's power. Do you have it?

Notice where that power comes in relation to the balanced Christian life. If Christ is not your possession, He cannot be your pattern. If you are not in Christ, you cannot become like Christ. Second, if Christ is not your pattern, He cannot be your purpose. If you are not like Christ, you cannot come to know Christ. God only teaches those who are teachable, those who are humble before Him. Third, if Christ is not your purpose, He cannot be your power. If you do not know Christ, you cannot have His power. Why does God give you His power? He gives it in order to make balance in the Christian life a reality, to make you confident in Him, not in your own strength, and to put in you a desire to know Him. Those are the things He gives power for, because those are the things that glorify Him the most. The end result of that power will be stability, contentment, and joy. Do you have it?

What is the balance to your life? Is Christ your possession? Are you confident? Is Christ your pattern? Are you seeing selfishness rooted out from you? Is Christ your purpose? Are you becoming intimate with Him? Is Christ your power? Are you finding peace, contentment, and joy in living for Him?

Philippians tells us the results of such balance in our lives: adversity will mean advance (1:12); conflict will bring confidence (1:14); rivalry will generate rejoicing (1:18–19); and death will resolve a dilemma (1:21). Surely, that balance is what we are pursuing. We might not have it fully yet, but we press on.

Blessed is the man who is so unattached to this world, that death is seen as a real dilemma. "For to me, to live is Christ, and to die is gain." Should we stay in order to be used of God, or should we go to meet Him with whom we belong? Only someone with a strong knowledge of who God is could even face such a question as Paul did.

May God bless you as you find your security in Him alone.

Prayer: Dear Lord, is my heart tuned to You to give what I cannot keep to gain what I cannot lose? Am I driven by that desire to know You? Sometimes I find I am, and then other times I sense a drifting heart. I know the answer to that balance, purpose, and power is not in me. I choose to get my eyes off of myself and look to You. I have learned that the answer to my deepest concerns is in the knowledge of You. As I continue in my discovery course of Your person, I rest in the great fact that You can do in me exactly what You did in the apostle Paul. What a model! I look to You to mold me in Your image. Thank You for revealing Yourself to me.

STUDY GUIDE

INTRODUCTION

We talk a lot today about loving and serving God more diligently, but both are impossible unless we first know Him. Though many Christians claim to know Him through a relationship with His Son, the Lord Jesus Christ, their knowledge is limited. They understand and experience little of His character, being, or motivations, and thus imperfectly worship Him, much less love or serve Him.

This book helps you to truly know the God of the Scriptures and understand your position in Christ. The study guide is intended to help you move from simply receiving new information to examining how it relates to your relationship with God, past and present. The purpose is to help you grow in your relationship with God from here on.

Before each question I have restated an important principle from the chapter to make it easier to understand the context of the question. The question is meant for you to personalize and apply that principle to your own life. May God bring you ever closer to truly knowing Him in the process.

JAMES S. BELL, JR.

CHAPTER ONE

If we do not have a true love relationship with God, we will worship and love other things in His place.

What earthly loves stand in the place of God in your life today and why?

The things you set your mind on most will shape your entire character and effect your eternal destiny.

What connection can you make between the things that most occupy your thinking and the quality of your behavior?

Remorse is mere sorrow for sin and its negative consequences, but repentance is viewing sin in the light of God's character.

Define your typical attitude to your own sins. Does it focus mainly on how it affects you or is it based on God's perspective?

CHAPTER TWO

Though we turn away from God, we can never rob Him of
His glory or defeat His purposes.

If we cannot subtract from God's glory, how can we enhance
it by our true worship and obedience?

When God's desires for us match our desires for Him, there
is an explosion of the reality of God's glory in our lives.

When have you sought God with all your heart for something that was His delight and you experienced a strong
sense of His presence or blessing?

We should seek discernment from God in every area of our
lives to determine if we are bringing Him glory—if not, we
should cease that activity.

Review those areas in your attitudes, desires, and activities
in terms of bringing God glory, and seek to make the necessary improvements.

CHAPTER THREE

Knowing a lot about God does not substitute for knowing him personally; for we cannot love or serve Him without knowing Him first.

When in your life has knowing teachings about God taken the place of an intimate relationship with Him? How can you change that?

God knows us completely, including our sinful behavior, and yet still loves us perfectly.

Be honest with God today about the things that keep you from Him, because He knows them anyway and can help you to grow closer to Him.

God's sovereign power causes all of his attributes to work together, so there is no inconsistency in His intentions or actions.

When have you seen more than one of God's attributes clearly at work in your own life—such as His justice and mercy? When has this harmony seemed difficult to understand?

CHAPTER FOUR

Only a God of perfect patience would put up with our sin for so long, but God wants us to repent so that we can experience His love for eternity.

Give God thanks for the times when you did not reap immediate consequences for your sin, but God gave you time to learn lessons and change your ways.

God's grace makes us as pure as God Himself but it comes with the greatest price tag ever: the cost of the life of His only Son.

What does the above statement mean to you in relation to all your problems, weaknesses, and sins? How does His grace go beyond your initial conversion experience?

God's wrath is actually comforting to the believer, who is restrained from sin by the knowledge that God's holiness will be displayed in future punishment.

How has both the fear of present consequences and future punishment kept you from further sin and given you a healthy respect for God?

CHAPTER FIVE

The cross is certainly about forgiveness and love, but it is also about the awful confrontation between holiness and sin.

How does what God has done on the cross for you enter into your perception of His holiness and your sin?

The cross was a war on sin launched on our behalf, setting us free from Satan's slavery and making us slaves to Christ.

Slavery usually has negative connotations, but what great benefits result from being a slave to the cause of Christ? What do you need to do reach this level of commitment?

No one suffered more conflict with sin and Satan than Jesus, but as a result God can totally reveal Himself to us.

When have you thought God was absent or didn't care? Meditate on the facts of what he did to break down all barriers and thank Him for His tremendous grace.

CHAPTER SIX

We may have many wrong concepts of God, such as the idea that He is motivated by what we give Him monetarily.

List some things you think motivate and please God in terms of how you respond to Him. Based on His sovereignty and power, how might your view be limited or misleading?

The relationship between the Father and His Son Jesus Christ are perfect examples of love within a family context.

What aspects of the Father and His Son in Scripture particularly attract you in terms of how you can be a better parent and /or child in your own family?

We are called to enjoy God forever, not as a distant commander or teacher, but as a loving Father who forgives our failures.

Overall, what is your concept of God as He relates to you? Do you perceive a Father who wants to lavish you with every good gift?

CHAPTER SEVEN

Though what we need most is intimate communication with God for His own sake, we are often motivated by our own personal needs in prayer.

How have your own problems and needs eventually led you into a deeper understanding and appreciation for God himself?

True worship of God always implies that we get rid of our pride, realizing that all we possess comes from Him.

In what ways has your pride come between you and God? How has he humbled you in the past to bring you closer to Him?

It is vital to spend time with the Lord, giving back to Him all your "crowns" (achievements) out of gratitude that He gave you the abilities in the first place.

As you tell God what it is you love about Him, list the achievements and benefits you may not have fully given back to Him, but may have selfishly enjoyed. Give them over to Him for His glory.

CHAPTER EIGHT

There are five key words used in Scripture to describe our salvation: justification, redemption, reconciliation, forgiveness, and sonship.

Based on the definitions given in the chapter, which of the five is best understood and received? Which do you least comprehend? In the latter case, apply yourself to more study and prayer.

To be "in Christ" means that we are completed spiritually. We need nothing more because he has completed our salvation on the cross.

When have you felt that you were not acceptable to God, and needed to do more to be pleasing to Him? Review the Scriptures about who Jesus is and why you are complete in Him. Ask Him to let you experience this at a deeper level.

Our sins do not change our relationship with God but forgiveness allows us to begin again on a daily basis.

Ask God to show you any unconfessed sin in your life and thank Him that by being cleansed nothing stands in the way of knowing Him better.

CHAPTER NINE

The hope of your calling in Christ is to ultimately inherit the great riches of His Kingdom, and to know that even now we are rich in Him.

Do you believe you have already obtained your spiritual inheritance in Christ? How can you better enjoy and use the great gifts that are yours as a believer as described in Philippians 1 and 2?

Some Christians put an emphasis on a life of rules to be obeyed rather than having a heart overflowing with thankfulness to the One who pours out His love to them.

Do you judge yourself and your closeness to God more on broken rules than on your experience of His love based on His Word? Thank Him for all He has done for you.

At times we tend to complain if we don't receive things from God that are actually bigger than we deserve, and when we don't realize our desires our thankfulness diminishes.

The apostle Paul was content with what he received because he knew he deserved nothing. Thank God for all you have received and seek Him for a spirit of contentment.

CHAPTER TEN

Because we are in Christ we can have confidence that no mater what the situation, God is in control and will bring good out of it.

Are you facing a situation where your confidence is shaken? Remember who you are in Christ and seek His grace based upon that sure foundation.

We sometimes think that the Christian life consists of trying our hardest to be like Christ; but rather, it is Christ living His life through us that allows us to achieve the goals God has for us.

When has the idea of imitating Christ caused you to try it on your own power rather than His? How can you let go and let the Lord do it through you?

Philippians 2 lists five deadly sins along side the need for humility. They are: apathy, selfishness, lack of quietness, lack of hatred for sin, and pride.

Try to come up with one simple statement as to how humility can overcome each of the five deadly sins above.

CHAPTER ELEVEN

Apathy, lack of purpose, and lack of creativity thwart the growth of the church, yet God has given each of us unique talents to use for a special purpose on His behalf.

Do you have a clear understanding of your purpose in the Body of Christ? As God makes that even clearer, commit to exercise vision and creativity as you serve Him.

God's vision for us is always something bigger and better, if we are willing to let go of what we have to obtain it.

Have you been unwilling at times to lose security or comfort in order to gain something better? Ask God to reveal His bigger and better plan for you and give you the grace to let go.

The result of knowing God's power is a greater confidence in prayer, a peace that goes beyond our comprehension, and a deeper appreciation for what He has given us.

Are you rejoicing and thanking God for all that you have obtained in Christ? Pray for the ability to accept whatever God brings your way with an open heart and hand.